CHRIST
and
CRISIS
in SOUTHEAST
ASIA

edited by
Gerald H. Anderson

S0-AXK-459

FRIENDSHIP PRESS   NEW YORK

Library of Congress Catalog Card Number: 68-14057

CONTENTS

SOME BASIC FACTS ABOUT SOUTHEAST ASIA

COUNTRY	AREA (SQUARE MILES)	CAPITAL	POPULATION (MILLIONS)	OFFICIAL LANGUAGE	MAJOR RELIGION	PROTESTANT COMMUNITY	CHRISTIAN PERCENTAGE OF POPULATION
BURMA	261,789	Rangoon	25	Burmese	Buddhism	750,000	4%
CAMBODIA	69,898	Phnom Penh	6	Cambodian (Khmer)	Buddhism	2,000	1%
INDONESIA	738,865	Djakarta	112	Indonesian	Islam	5,000,000	6.3%
LAOS	91,000	Vientiane and Luang Prabang	3	Lao	Buddhism	11,000	2%
MALAYSIA (E & W)	128,308	Kuala Lumpur	10	Malay	Islam	180,000	3.3%
and SINGAPORE	225	Singapore	2	Malay	Buddhism		
PHILIPPINES	115,758	Quezon City and Manila	35	Pilipino (Tagalog)	Roman Catholicism	1,020,000	92%
THAILAND	200,148	Bangkok	30	Thai	Buddhism	30,000	0.5%
VIETNAM (North)	62,000	Hanoi	18	Annamese	Buddhism	no figure available	3%
VIETNAM (South)	65,000	Saigon	16	Annamese	Buddhism	150,000	10%

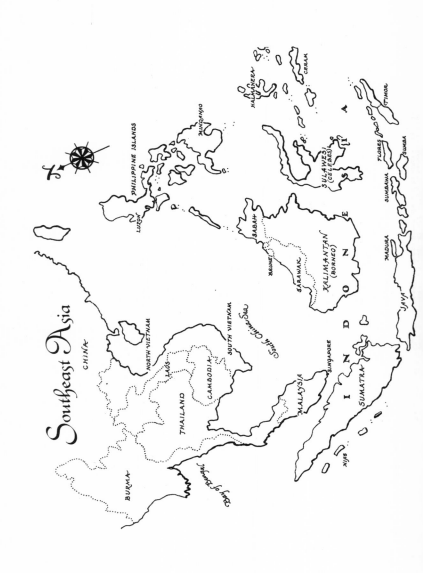

Southeast Asia

CHRIST and CRISIS
in SOUTHEAST ASIA

INTRODUCTION

SOUTHEAST ASIA lies in a geographic arc of continuing crisis. Its territory includes the area east from Burma and west from the Philippines, south from the border of China and north from the islands of Indonesia. Within this tropical area, which straddles the equator, live 257 million people in 10 independent states (Burma, Thailand, Cambodia, Laos, North and South Vietnam, Singapore, Malaysia, Indonesia and the Philippines), and two remaining colonial possessions (Portuguese Timor and the British Protected Sultanate of Brunei).

One of the distinctive features of Southeast Asia is the diversity of its peoples and cultures. Despite some common physical, mental and cultural characteristics, such as color, size, ethnic origin, food, housing and social organization, there are important differences among the various national groups and peoples, notably in language and religion. They speak with a thousand tongues, and Southeast Asia has been called "the crossroad of religions."

Two factors behind the current ferment are of primary importance. First is the radical impact of *modernization,* of rapid social change in Southeast Asia. Events which in the West were spread over the last four centuries have been telescoped into four decades in Asia. This modernization, which is not identical with Westernization, has involved the breaking up of traditional patterns of life and thought and the developing of new structures for society and a new style of living, based on technology, secularization and humanism. The transformation and transition now in process from the old to the new is exciting and explosive.

Second is the force of *nationalism,* an intensification of the self-conscious assertion of human dignity and national identity, the desire for independence and equality. This force provides the momentum for modernization and is itself fed by an animosity toward Western imperialism and exploitation in any measure or form—political, economic, military or religious. Throughout Southeast Asia, nationalism has led to revolution in virtually every realm of life. And "Asian revolution," as a noted American scholar has observed, "is the most dynamic factor in the history of the twentieth century." [1] Nationalism, as the bearer of revolution in Southeast Asia, requires the most careful consideration by the Christian church, which is itself the bearer of a revolutionary gospel.

[1] Claude A. Buss, *The Arc of Crisis: Nationalism and Neutralism in Asia Today.* Garden City: Doubleday & Co., 1961, p. 19. I am also indebted here to Dr. Richard L. Deats and Dr. Emerito P. Nacpil, for sharing with me some of their observations.

With the exception of the Philippines, Christianity is definitely a minority faith in Southeast Asia. Approximately 15 percent of the entire population in the region is Christian of any persuasion; 2.8 percent is Protestant. The church is still "a tiny David confronting an enormous Goliath of non-Christian religions and cultures, of communism and increasing secularism." [2] The church is established in every land of Southeast Asia, but it remains to be seen in the following chapters to what extent the Christian presence—usually with a fragmented gospel and an inwardly divided community—has exerted an influence in the region.

Two fundamental problems have consistently plagued the churches. First, as one Asian has expressed it, "Christianity is largely a 'potted plant' in Southeast Asia. It has been transported without being transplanted. It is still viewed by Asians as a foreign importation and imposition." This sentiment has been strengthened with the rise of nationalism and the resurgence of non-Christian religions. The fact that Christianity began in Asia does not matter; it traveled to Southeast Asia by way of the West. The challenge remains for the churches to relate themselves more fully to the soil of Southeast Asia—to get down to the rice-roots level of Asian civilization.

The second problem is that Christians have tended toward a ghetto mentality among themselves. A Catholic writer has observed that the Christian community has been more like glue than leaven. The churches have been preoccupied with their own existence and organization, and correspondingly they have lagged behind in prophetic concern for the social relevance and outreach of the gospel into

[2] Rajah B. Manikam and Winburn T. Thomas, *The Church in Southeast Asia*. New York: Friendship Press, 1956, p. 157.

the mainstream task of nation building. At best, in the view of one missionary: "The churches have been more resolutionary than revolutionary in their approach to the social problems of Southeast Asia; they have said more than they have done." Part of the reason for this isolation from national life has been a minority consciousness among many Christians, with an accompanying sense of security (and perhaps superiority) achieved by insulating themselves against involvement. Another part has been a pietistic heritage, which does not take social struggles seriously. In many instances, however, it has been a lack neither of courage nor of conviction. Rather, lack of understanding and knowledge about the dynamics of social change and the development of new forms of witness and service has kept Christians from responsible participation in the social problems inherent in the contemporary Asian revolution.

In recent years the churches in Southeast Asia have been grappling afresh with both of these problems—and a host of related issues—in a constructive and promising fashion. The problems have not been resolved, but significant advances have been achieved. The chapters that follow discuss the developments and circumstances of the churches in each of the countries, beginning with Burma in the west and ending with the Philippines in the east. All the contributing writers have lived and worked with the churches in Southeast Asia for many years. They represent a diverse background of nationalities and Christian traditions, but they share a common conviction of the Lordship of Jesus Christ and the urgency of his mission in revolutionary Southeast Asia.

GERALD H. ANDERSON

1 BURMA

the church amid the pagodas

Paul Clasper

The Burmese are "The Irish of the East."

Burma has a different quality from other Asian countries; there is a lilt to life here; the people instinctively smile.

In Burma you find classical Buddhism in its finest form.

Of all the students we met in America we liked those guys from Texas best; they were just like us Burmese.

RANDOM REMARKS do not tell the whole story of a country, though they are sometimes significant pointers. A balanced view of Burma requires a combination of often conflicting pictures and impressions: A country of remarkably friendly people, Burma is today virtually closed to outsiders; this well-known Buddhist stronghold is politically integrated by a military-socialist regime; and the land where the monsoons never fail, which formerly exported more rice than its two chief rivals combined, has recently suffered from a severe rice shortage.

Since July 13, 1813, when Ann and Adoniram Judson, America's first missionaries to Asia, sailed up the Rangoon River, there has been a special link between Burma and America, especially through the Christian church. In a stream of letters and writings from Burma, Americans began to learn their first lessons in missionary education. To this day the study of Burma is especially rewarding, for it can give us an understanding both of a rapidly changing Asia and of the Christian mission in the midst of the Asian ferment.

THE LAND OF BUDDHISM, RICE AND U THANT

Burma is known as "the land of rice and spice, peacocks and pagodas." Many Europeans add, "mosquitoes and malaria." In numerous ways Burma could qualify as "a pulsebeat of Asia." A country roughly the size of Texas with approximately 25 million people, situated between China and India, its life is a unique blend of elements from each cultural heritage. Most of the tribal or racial groups found in Burma have Mongolian features and originated in Central China. The Burmese spoken language is tonal and monosyllabic, like Chinese, but the written language uses an alphabet derived from the eastern coast of India. The dominant religion, Buddhism, came from India by way of Ceylon.

Burma's economy depends on the production and export

of rice. Unlike many Asian countries it has through the years been well fed. Indians, in the past, longed to migrate to Burma as a lush land of easy living. Until very recently the Burmese have had little interest in migrating to other countries—after all, if you live in Burma why go elsewhere? The symbol of Burma is the proud peacock.

Burma is "typical" in history and politics. Early history reveals numerous small kingdoms and dynasties attempting to establish control over the country. In 1886 the British annexed Burma, and it became part of British India. Many of the tribal minority peoples thought of the colonial period as a time of opportunity and justice; but the majority, the Burmese, became increasingly restless under foreign rule. Movements for independence became strong in the early 1930's and up to World War II. During the war Burma experienced Japanese occupation, but in 1948 Burma achieved independence and became the Republic of the Union of Burma.

Since Independence the country has struggled through civil war and unrest, seeking to unite the great diversity of peoples within its borders. It has attempted to combine the best insights of a renewed Buddhism with the help of a Marxist-Socialist reordering of society. U Nu, Prime Minister until 1962, combined many of the functions of the old Burmese kings in taking the initiative to purify and propagate the Buddhist Way. General Ne Win, in recent years, has given a military efficiency (not exactly natural to the Burmese temperament) to a predominantly secular program of socialism. Burma's best known world-citizen, U Thant, Secretary General of the United Nations, was a quiet, scholarly, small-town school teacher until his entry into political life in independent Burma.

It is easy to see why Adoniram Judson felt that the mission of the Christian church met a strategic challenge in Burma. Today the challenge is even more pointed. In the face of a renewed and resurgent Buddhism and the people's choice of socialism as a viable way of ordering the political and economic life, what does it mean for the church to witness to the "new life in Christ"? What is this new life for both "religious man" and "secular man" in Asia today? *What is the task of the Christian missionary (national or foreign) in the land of pagodas?*

THE CHURCH AMID THE PAGODAS

Judson labored for seven years before he baptized the first Burmese convert, U Naw. After spending his life spreading the Christian gospel among the Buddhist-background Burmese, Judson summed up the situation realistically: "It is easier to extract a tooth from the tiger's mouth than to convert a Burmese Buddhist to the Christian faith." In the face of incredible discouragements he persisted in his hope that "the day will come when the hillsides of Burma, now studded with pagodas, will be filled with the towers of Christian churches."

Today, a little more than 150 years since Judson's arrival, there are hundreds of churches on the hillsides and thousands of Christians among the animist-background tribal peoples. There are still relatively few Christians among the Burmese of Buddhist background. If statistics alone are taken as the criterion (to be sure, the poorest way to evaluate the vitality of the Christian movement), they would seem to show that Burma is at the same time one of the most difficult and one of the most successful fields of Christian missionary activity.

The largest minority group in Burma is a tribal people known as the Karens. For centuries these shy, backward hill people had lived with a sense of inferiority to the dominant Burmese. They were animists (worshiping the spirits in the trees, mountains, or rivers), not Buddhists. Each generation, however, had been nourished on the hope that one day a white brother would come in a large boat and bring them a golden book that would lead them back to God and a whole new way of life. This seemed to the early missionaries like a soil prepared for the seed of the gospel. Before long Karens had become Christians in great numbers. Today, numerically speaking, the church among the Karens is one of the largest and strongest Christian groups in Asia.

Other tribal groups have also responded. The second largest group of Christians is found among the Kachin tribes, who live along the China border. And there are also strong churches among the Chins (along the India border), the Lahus (along the Thailand border) and numerous other groups. All these Christian groups have able national leadership, nationally staffed Bible schools and seminaries and ambitious programs of education, agricultural improvement, and refugee and resettlement aid. The Burma Christian Council and the Burma Baptist Convention (the two largest and most diversified associations of Christians in the country) include representatives from more than 20 different language groups.

Among the Burmese of Buddhist background, the church continues to be numerically small; but this group has an importance out of all proportion to its size. It is not surprising that many able leaders have emerged from this group to serve not only the church in Burma but the wider ecumenical fellowship. U Ba Hmyin, Secretary of the Burma Baptist Churches Union, gave the keynote address at the World Council of Churches Assembly in New Delhi in 1961; Dr. Hla Bu, then professor of philosophy at Rangoon University, was visiting professor at Union Theological Seminary in New York; U Kyaw Than has served in the secretariat of the East Asia Christian Conference; U Pe Maung Tin, first Burmese Rector of Rangoon University and noted Buddhist scholar, was a visiting professor at the University of Chicago.

This vivid contrast between the phenomenal response of the hill people and the meager response of the Buddhist population raises deep questions about the church and its mission. Anthropologists are quick to point out that some peoples and situations are ripe for change and others are not. The church has grown numerically where the conditions were such that a radical change was wanted and possible. Is this a strategy of "going where the picking is easy" or wisely responding to an open-door opportunity? Is it in line with Jesus' ironical saying that only the sick, not the well, need the doctor? But what of the Christian responsibility, as well as methodology, for witness to the deeply rooted Buddhist? The German theologian of the past generation, Ernst Troeltsch, contended that Christianity was the soul of the West but should not be intruded into the Orient, which had its own distinct soul in Hinduism and Buddhism. He did grant that Christianity might have a mission among the culturally deprived minority groups. In some ways this has been the way it has worked out so far in Burma. But how is the aim of mission to be thought of and realized in the light of a Christian faith that believes it is universal (ecumenical, catholic); that is, meant for all men and capable of being lived in all cultures and periods? In what sense is Christian faith meant "for all"?

Two of the most striking features of the church in Burma are its diversity of peoples and cultures and the high quality of leadership found at all levels. This diversity is the great glory and at times the great despair of Burma, in both the church and the political spheres.

Literature must be translated into many, many languages if it is to reach people "in their own tongue." The whole Bible is translated into six of the major languages and parts of the Bible are available in more than 20 other languages. The great extension of Burmese, however, is now making possible a common language that all educated people can use. The church must be hearing and answering the questions both of tribal people who wonder wistfully if the earth is really round, and of professors with PhD's in science and psychology. The generation gap is wide here. A village pastor does a good job with little education, while his son is working on his third university degree. Some live where the Iron Age is just beginning and others where a cosmopolitan secularism is the real world. To find and express the unity in Christ here is both exhilarating and patience-demanding!

The training of Christian leadership has been emphasized in Burma from the beginning. Early missionaries gathered leaders on their porches during the five-month rainy season (which occurs at the same time as the Buddhist Lent, when the monks travel less and live closer to the monasteries). From this practice has emerged a system of graded Bible schools and seminaries in several languages as well as the Burma Divinity School, located five miles out of

Rangoon on the Insein Road (or as the local people call it, "The Road of a Thousand Smells"). Well-educated laymen have played a conspicuous role in the life of the church and the country. Christians have been especially active in the fields of education, medicine and social service.

All remaining foreign missionaries were asked by the government to leave Burma in 1966. The action was not unduly abrupt, for foreigners in other positions had been asked to leave even earlier. Through many years of preparation, the church has achieved a rather high level of trained indigenous leadership. In recent years missionaries have been "helpers," but the leadership of institutions, such as high schools, seminaries and hospitals, has already been in the hands of experienced Burmese. Some of the finest words of appreciation for this strategy have come from Roman Catholics, who have been much slower to develop a responsible national leadership. Many of them have said, "You Protestants were wise, and in the future we must do more of what you have done in Burma." Protestants should not indulge in self-congratulation; but such a willingness to learn and to assess work realistically, not defensively, is one of the brightest signs of the ecumenical era that is just opening.

The relationship of unity and diversity underlies every aspect of life in Burma. It is not surprising that the concerns of the ecumenical era have long been alive in Burma, and the church there is seeking to express its unity in Christ in its own way. In many respects the church in Burma is remarkably united, though there have been no great efforts toward achieving an organizationally "united church."

The church is composed of several historic traditions. Statistics can only be roughly suggestive, but the approximate relative size of some of the various communions is as follows: Baptists 500,000; Roman Catholics 250,000; Church of England 18,000; Methodists 12,000; Seventh-Day Adventists 5,000. In a population of roughly 25 million, Christians constitute about 4 percent.

With the great preponderance of Baptists, and with the next highest Protestant group being the Church of England, it is not easy to visualize an organic church union in quite the form that is urged in some areas. One of the questions is whether the aim in church unity is some pattern that will come to be accepted as "standard" or whether unity must be worked out in local situations, according to the needs and factors in each area? If the latter, unity becomes a question of what vision of goal and method is operating.

The relatively simple, flexible ways of Baptist church polity are easily adaptable to the variety of frontier situations in Burma. On the other hand, the rich traditions of Anglican worship are greatly needed. In a country like Burma it would surely be hoped that a rich and flexible diversity might always be encouraged in the church. Nevertheless the need for unity in witness and service is crucial. At the present time the Burma Christian Council is an instrument for a high degree of united worship and work. Vatican II has made possible many new, potentially fruitful relationships between Roman Catholic and Protestant groups. Through such organizations as the East Asia Christian Conference and the Association of Theological Schools in Southeast Asia, Christians in Burma are linked in learning and serving relationships with other Asian Christians across racial and denominational lines. Ironically enough, these lines are opening at the very time when Burma is closing herself to the outside world.

The shape Christian unity will take in Burma cannot be predicted. There are many reasons to believe that it will be a specifically Burmese shape, not simply the application of a set form, devised elsewhere and pressed upon the Burma situation. But there is always the danger of accepting and perpetuating old tribal-denominational differences long after their usefulness has been outgrown. Fostering the tribal mentality, instead of facing the demands of a new day, can easily mark church groups (even large ones) as relics of yesterday, rather than as signs of God's creative activity in the present.

It is easy to be lethargic in Burma. The climate is conducive to taking it very easy!

CHALLENGE AND RESPONSE

Arnold Toynbee has taught us to see the vitality of a culture by looking at its capacity for creative response to the challenges of history. Such a framework is a convenient lens through which to view three of the pressing challenges Christians face in Burma today.

Buddhism and an Authentic Asian Church

In the Land of Pagodas the Christian faith must live and think in relationship to one of the great traditions of Buddhism. Burmese Buddhism represents the Theravada Buddhist tradition; that is, the "Way of the Elders." This is the classic, conservative, scriptural type of Buddhism which is found also in Ceylon, Thailand, Cambodia and Laos. The Buddha believed the truth of enlightenment to consist of a realistic facing of suffering and frustration, and a disciplined middle path of self-effort leading to Nirvana, or Emancipation. He warned against the illusion of a slave-like dependence on gods or outside sources of help. His final words summed up the essence of his teaching: "Be ye lamps unto yourselves. Go to no external refuge. Look not for refuge to any one besides yourselves. Decay is inherent in all things. Work out your salvation with diligence."

The Burmese blame the British for much of the recent decline in Buddhist vitality. Buddhism thrives on state sponsorship but suffers when it lacks governmental patronage. Consequently, the rise of nationalism has also seen the revival of Buddhism. Today, to be an "authentic Burmese" means to be a Buddhist. When it comes to dress, one should either dress Burmese or Western, but not half and half. Likewise, Burmese feel, if one is an Asian he should live by the Asian faith, Buddhism. "Christianity is for Westerners and Karens," one often hears.

But Christian faith has refused to think of itself as solely a Western faith. It is universal; *it is meant for all.* How then does it see itself in relationship to the Buddha, known as "The Light of Asia"?

On the whole, Christians "have resolved to preach the gospel, not anti-Buddhism." But the question of relationship can neither be ignored nor solved with a glib formula. From one standpoint, it can be hoped that the highest and best of the Buddhist Way can be taken up, baptized and used to infuse the Christian Way with some enriching elements. Christianity has always been a learning-absorbing faith, as well as a witnessing-preaching faith.

On the other hand, there is a deep, basic difference that cannot be smoothed over without peril to an understanding of both faiths. One faith describes a way of enlightenment-emancipation by self-effort; the ideal is the Arahant, the saint, who achieves detachment from the defilement of the world. The other describes new life in the midst of the old. It points to the cross as the symbol of a necessary, costly involvement and identification with the world. It points to the ideal of "ambassadors for Christ," who live fully in the midst of the old world but also act as representatives of the new world. Life here is based on gratitude and the good news of the possibility of the new life which comes from God through Christ.

There can be no doubt that the Christian in Burma today must wrestle with the question of the relationship of the two lights—the Light of Asia and the Light of the World. It is no longer possible for Christians to ride the comfortable crest of the colonial era. The Christian is called to be *both* culturally appreciative *and* faithful to the gospel. The Christian community must not be alienated from the broad Asian heritage, which could well enrich its own understanding and practice of the Christian faith and be a part of its special contribution to the world Christian community.

One example may suffice. In Asia generally and in Burma particularly, meditation is an art that is cultivated with great devotion and precision. The meditation center is as much a part of Burma as the rice field and the tea shop. It might be reasonable to hope that the prayer life of Burmese Christians would reflect something of this capacity for "the time of quiet" and a "disciplined waiting," which need not be a retreat from life but an inner preparation for creative living. But here the Protestant churches simply reflect the traditions that have come to them; and frequently such traditions are impervious to any appreciation of what is often disparagingly called "mysticism."

Might this be a small part of the large Asian heritage that should not be resisted, but utilized, for the enrichment of Asian Christians and for the world Christian community? It is necessary to pray with St. Francis: "Help me not so much to seek to be understood, as to understand." And it is also necessary to say with St. Paul: "Woe is me if I preach not the gospel."

"The Burmese Way to Socialism" *and a Worldly Christianity*

At least on the surface, the influence of Karl Marx is even more important in today's Burma than that of the Lord Buddha. Since Independence, much of Burma's social and political thinking has drawn heavily on Marxist interpretations. This is not to say Burma has longed for communism. She has stubbornly resisted being drawn into either Communist or non-Communist alignment. Her policy of neutralism means doing things her own way, without help or interference from those who would like to woo her to their side.

The present military government is much more concerned with improving social conditions than with spreading Buddhism. Banks, businesses, schools and hospitals have all been nationalized with a view to stabilizing the economy and spreading the good things of life more widely among the peasants. This program is called "The Burmese Way to Socialism."

As a result, the most familiar means by which Christians have witnessed to their faith—mission schools, hospitals and agricultural stations—are no longer church-operated but state-sponsored. Does this mean that Christian witness is deprived of its opportunity? Or must that witness simply find new structures and forms for expression? Christians have been doing much heart-searching to discover new modes of witness which are possible and relevant in a Socialist regime. Many wish for a return to "the good old days." The more adventuresome are trying to find new shapes of ministry for a rapidly and radically changing society.

In some ways Christians are better prepared than Buddhists for relating their faith to social service concerns. There is the long tradition of Christian participation in the social services, in contrast to the general drift away from involvement that has characterized classical Buddhism.

Yet Christians cannot be smug. Much of the church life in Burma has also tended to a quietistic withdrawal from the political sphere. Christians have not been schooled in the ways of power politics and the place of revolution in changing the structures of society. To be sure, they have often participated in revolutions. But they have done so with no clear understanding of how these are related to Christian social witness and responsible living in a society interpreted largely in Marxist categories.

Much of the future of the church will depend on whether it is able to learn the new lessons fast enough to live with any kind of relevance in a secular-Socialist world. For this Marxist-Socialist world is fast becoming a more real world for Asians than the traditional Buddhist world. *Christian dialogue with Asian Marxism is every bit as urgent as the confrontation with Buddhism.*

The New Nation and the Community of Grace

Burma's quest for national selfhood is related to what has just been said. To bring the variety of peoples into some working unity, with a sense of national identity and purpose and not simply an artificially imposed law, is a major task of long-range priority. In the past, various Burmese kings sought to achieve control. The *Pax Britannica* produced a working unity for a period. Since Independence the majority people, the Burmese, have sought to weld a unity through the extension of a common language, the government educational system and the promotion of the Buddhist heritage. Still, the hill peoples refer to a trip to Mandalay as "going down to Burma." They do not think of themselves as belonging to Burma in a significant way. Since the Karen Rebellion (or Civil War) in 1950, the Kachins, Chins, Shans and other groups have in varying degrees resisted the strengthening of the "Union" of Burma.

In this process of tribal dynamics the church in Burma has a difficult role, a role that is not altogether clear. Because the church is found largely among the tribal peoples, it might be easy for the Christian faith to become the rallying point for those who resist the Union in Burma. For those bent on creating some working political unity it is easy to view Christianity as a subtle source of restlessness and insurrection among the tribal peoples. Christian faith would probably bolster certain loyalties and criticize others. But often these loyalties are as tangled and jumbled as the Burmese jungle itself.

Christians in Burma are not likely to confuse serving the kingdom of God with serving the central government. They are more likely to set the two apart at too great a distance. Many of the leading churchmen are ex-army officers from the British days. The contrast is sometimes stated that previously they worked for the army or the government; now they are working for the kingdom of God. The manner of being a responsible Christian is never easy; and it is peculiarly complex in Burma today.

There is no doubt that the Christian church has a great potential as a unifying factor, especially among the various tribal peoples. But how is the ministry of reconciliation to be expressed in political terms in the complexities of nation building? Christian existence in Burma will of necessity become increasingly a political existence in the days to come. Many new lessons will need to be learned, and the Christian's capacity for learning will be severely tested.

The Christian church is called upon to be a community of grace, living among and in touch with all the realities of today's world. It cannot be simply a pale reflection of the world about it, nor can it disengage itself in order to promote its own purity.

In Burma the church is called to be what M. M. Thomas of India has described as "the one personal reality in all Asia." He says that "if the missionary movement and the church in Asia continue to proclaim the transcendent Word of God and to be a Community of Grace in tension with the political, economic and social orders of Asia today and tomorrow, it will be the greatest contribution they can make to Asian society."

When Adoniram Judson was asked about the prospects for the gospel in Burma, his answer was a classic combination of realism and hope: "The future is as bright as the promises of God." In Burma the church has a good heritage and some stalwart leadership. The ground of hope, however, is not in the "arm of flesh" but in the "power of the Spirit," made manifest supremely in Jesus Christ and continuously operative in his body, the church.

2 THAILAND

a struggling church in a stable land

Ray C. Downs

FAR TO THE NORTHWEST of Bangkok, only a few miles from the Burma border, nestles a little village, Sangklaburi. The sun sparkles on a river, the River Kwai. Mist hangs heavy over the jungle hills; and teak forests, tropical and dank, drip with humidity. Down the river in a beautiful cemetery, thousands of crosses mark the places of those who labored on the "Bridge on the River Kwai." Sun shines, steam rises, over a new little Christian outpost. The fences for the ten-bed Christian hospital are made of the disintegrating railroad ties of World War II infamy. Each tie, according to stories still circulating, cost a human life.

But all is not peace, even a quarter of a century later. Bands of dissident soldiers from Burma and Nationalist

China, along with current revolutionaries and feuding tribal groups, roam the mountains of the far north. Behind the deep quiet of the jungle churn the resentments, the centuries-old conflicts, the yearning for new revolution. There the church takes root.

So far away that it appears to be another world, yet only a hundred miles away, Bangkok, "City of Angels," sprawls over the mudflats of the Chao Phraya River delta. In a decade the city has doubled its size to two million. Yesterday oarsmen threaded their boats through the canals, the main thoroughfares in this Venice of the East; today hundreds of thousands of automobiles battle for space on its wide boulevards and thruways. Once an occasional visitor climbed down the gangplank of a tramp freighter; now thousands of tourists per week drop from the skies to fill its luxury hotels. And throughout this land, fiercely independent for more than seven centuries, American soldiers and American military equipment build, fly, prepare and fortify.

There is a throbbing, pulsating note to the bursting Thai economy. Buffalo carts still creak along rutted paths, but an endless stream of trucks and buses now pound along great highways. Bicycles give way to the Honda, the lonely flute to the electric guitar. Even in the rice paddies the transistor radio sets the rhythm of the hoe. The gross national product will have doubled in less than 20 years—and the Thai think that rate is too slow. But there is still much to be done. The per capita income in the parched northeast is only one-seventh of what it is in the central plains.

The recently dedicated Phumipol Dam in the far north, named after the reigning king, is the sixth-largest in the world. Electricity from its massive generators runs machinery 600 miles away. Its irrigation channels distribute water over hundreds of square miles of cracked and arid land.

The great Mekong River project is the one project upon which the frequently squabbling Thailand, Laos, Cambodia and the Republic of Vietnam seem able to agree. A vast four-nation TVA, it promises to do far more to bring peace and security to this area than armies and treaties.

In the midst of all this upheaval, one finds the Christian church, small and sometimes lost in the hurly-burly. But it is there, providing a measure of continuity with the past, pointing an occasional finger to the future. Whether on the farthest outpost in a tiny hospital, on a busy street corner or in the factories of the city, the church is a part of an emerging new Thailand.

AN ANCIENT NATION

How did this nation begin? Where did its people come from? The earliest Thai tribes were probably driven down from China about 2,000 years ago. The prelude to modern Thailand, however, dates to the middle of the thirteenth century when the Thai battled the Cambodians and, on the basis of their new-found freedom, established their own capital at Sukothai under King Indrathit. His son, the legendary King Ramkamhaeng, extended this kingdom all the way down the southern peninsula to Malaysia. He not only set up a functioning government, but he also laid down the first body of Thai law, set the Thai language into writing and laid the foundations for a new culture. Great potteries shipped their products as far as Indonesia, and ambassadors were received by the king from the courts of Asia. Throughout the thirteenth and early fourteenth centuries, Siam gathered to itself the disintegrating fragments of Cambodian culture; then enshrined this culture, with even more brilliance, in a new capital at Ayuthia, founded in A.D. 1350. During this period, the borders of Siam were the widest in its history and the culture of the country reached a peak never again attained.

Then came the first contacts with the West. Portuguese commercial adventurers found their way up the Chao Phraya River to the exotic island capital of Ayuthia in 1511, and an era ended. They brought with them firearms, fortifications and Roman Catholicism. Then came the Dutch bringing the art of shipbuilding, and the English with the science of navigation and the bustle of commerce. The first missionary actually to reach the shores of Siam, a Roman Catholic priest, arrived in the year 1511; and Catholic missionaries have been in continuous residence since 1555. Quite unlike the later history of Protestant missions, theirs was spotted from the first by persecutions and deaths. After a century and a half of work, there were only about 600 Thai Christians. French priests arrived in force in the latter part of the seventeenth century hoping to convert Siam for the glory of King Louis and the Pope. These aspirations were cut short when the conversion of a Prime Minister aroused such consternation that it provoked a coup d'état and a wave of persecution.

In April, 1767, the old arch-enemy, Burma, descended on this extraordinary capital, utterly destroying it and almost as completely destroying the great culture it had expressed. Ancient Siam was gone. A band of soldiers escaped the carnage and fled down the river to encamp at what was to become Bangkok, and modern Thailand was born. King Rama there founded the monarchical line, which continues ith King Phumipol on the throne today as King Rama IX.

PROTESTANT BEGINNINGS

The first Protestant missionaries arrived in Siam in 1828, half-century after the founding of Bangkok. They moved with faith, with skills, with ingenuity and with no little ravery. Great even among these mighty pioneers was the ev. Dr. Dan Beach Bradley. Friend of royalty and commoner, he spent 38 years in Siam with only one home leave. Ie dared to try anything. As early as 1835, he attempted blood transfusion to save the life of a friend. In the same ear, he brought the first printing press to Siam. His first ublication was *The Ten Commandments*; and his first rinting for the king was an edict forbidding the use of pium. He performed the first surgical operation in Siam 1 1837 and followed that with the first inoculations and accinations against smallpox. He had to make his own accine from a scab embedded in a lump of beeswax rought with him from Boston—a nine-month sea journey. Ie edited the first newspaper in Thailand and his journal, rare historical document, is in safekeeping at the Oberlin ollege Library. It is little wonder that this physician, riter, translator, printer, preacher and scholar is one of e authentic heroes of Thai history and folklore, the subct of movies, TV shows and radio programs. Dr. Bradley rovides a preview of the breadth and variety of interests f the men who were to follow him and of the church at would bloom from their efforts.

It is hard to recapture, in this day of massive government id and loan programs, the influence exerted by individual issionaries in those earlier days. Advisors, teachers and iends to kings, queens and royal children, they enlarged

the thinking and liberalized the minds that opened Tha
land to the West. That Thailand had to confront the Wes
was a matter of historical inevitability. That it was pre
pared for the encounter by sympathetic and generou:
minded men was the earliest and one of the greatest con
tributions of the Christian church.

MODERN THAILAND

Nostalgia for the past can never completely obscur
harsh reality. The basic reality of modern Thailand, as o
its neighbors, is change—constant, seething, radica
fundamental change. Scarcely more than half a centur
ago, the king, reigning as absolute monarch, could and di
claim the heads of miscreant subjects. The political wate1
shed for Thailand came in 1932, with the overthrow of th
absolute monarchy by a coup d'état arranged by a grou
of young army officers trained in France. The Coup Party
as it came to be called, has controlled the political life o
the nation ever since. Attempts are still being made t
establish a constitutional democracy. But the present gov
ernment might best be called, "military junta." It is no
surprising that democracy takes root slowly, for centurie
of feudal authoritarianism are not easily expunged. It is a
easy error to assume that democracy is the only prope
form of government for all people at all times. Thailan
has achieved order, social responsibility and an advance
level of national development without democracy. It ha
even evolved a functioning solution to the trickiest politic;
problem, that of the transfer of power—by orderly cou
d'état.

With increasing awareness of nationhood, there appea1
its handmaiden, nationalism. Like every other problem be

deviling the modern world, nationalism takes on unique characteristics in every country. In Thailand, these are partly a result of the extraordinary success of foreign policy in recent centuries. While other nations were subjected to wave upon wave of colonial assault, Thailand managed, at rather modest cost in territory, to pick its way through the many threats to its national integrity. This experience seemed to endow the Thai with a healthy skepticism toward the motives of the great powers. At the same time, they avoided the excesses of xenophobic reaction, which breed the virus of intense nationalism. The Thai need carry no chip on the shoulder in their relationships with the West. They might graciously admit that other peoples may be almost as noble as the Thai people, though not quite. Free and easy tolerance of the idiosyncrasies of the West results.

Thus Christian workers from abroad enjoy a rather high degree of acceptance and nondiscrimination. Relationships between Christian missionaries and the Thai have always been friendly, even cordial. There are few of the resentments and pent-up hatreds sometimes found elsewhere. But clouds appear on the horizon. As Thai nationalism increases, patriotism and Buddhism sometimes tend to merge. The Thai Christian is proud of being Thai. He considers himself as patriotic and devoted a subject of the king as any other Thai. It hurts and troubles him to have his patriotism called into question because of his religious belief. This tension calls for special sensitivity on the part of the foreigner, who must be doubly careful not to parade his national origins.

Nor is that all. The numbers of Americans in Thailand since World War II have increased from a hundred or two to a figure gradually moving up to 100,000. In other words, Thailand is being inundated, and sensitivity increases. A Westerner, in Thailand, is called a "farang," a corruption of the Thai word for Frenchman, the early Westerners. The word increasingly carries a derisive connotation, and excessive association with farangs may be suspect. At the same time, Thai Christians are proud of their church's international connections. They debate among themselves, to be sure. One person will proclaim loudly for the eviction of all farangs, while another will answer with an equally impassioned plea that "you are all one in Christ Jesus." Some Christians from postcolonial nations find it hard to believe the relaxed relationship that exists between Thai and foreigner. The presence of the Christian church in Thailand has not only softened the impact of the West, it has tended to dull the harsh edges of nationalism. It has been a window on the world.

The American presence in Thailand is not temporary. It is easier to move hordes of troops in than to move them out. The presence of foreign troops in any nation is almost certain to cause irritation. This irritation will be reflected within the church itself, which feels a tension between its ecumenical commitments and the integrity of its own Thai witness. This witness presupposes Thai leadership. Despite the genuine desire of the Thai church to maintain its international relations, the day may be near when Westerners will be more of an irritant than a source of help. If that should happen, Asian fraternal workers will be able to help the Thai church to maintain its ecumenical relationships.

The East Asia Christian Conference and the World Council of Churches, of which the Church of Christ in Thailand is a member, will help to keep the sharp edges of provincialism from curling inward. It is this hope that spurs on efforts to provide the EACC with structure and flesh, for it may have to pick up more and more of the work formerly carried on by Western missions. With this new relationship, too, the church demonstrates the flexibility that makes possible a continuity of presence and witness through historical change and turmoil.

BIRTH OF A CHURCH

While Christianity is no newcomer to Thailand, the indigenous Thai church began to establish itself only in 1930 when the Siam National Christian Council was formed. Four years later the first General Assembly of the Church of Christ in Thailand took place. The Eleventh Assembly of the Church drew 140 delegates to Bangkok in December, 1966. Originally it was the hope that all Protestant bodies and work would be united in this endeavor. Only the Presbyterians and the Chinese Baptists actually joined, although the American Baptists cooperate in an affiliate relationship which is periodically restudied. The following groups have fully integrated their work in Thailand within the united church: The United Christian Missionary Society, the Marburger Mission, the United Church of Christ in the Philippines, the Church of South India, the Presbyterian Church of Korea, and the Kyodan of Japan. These groups have given meaning to the word "ecumenical." The presence of fraternal workers from India, Korea, Japan, Germany, Indonesia and the Philippines, when added to the Americans and English already there, lends dramatic and visible proof of the worldwide dimension of Christianity and makes it difficult for the Thai church to withdraw into the dark recesses of nationalism.

OLD AND NEW MISSIONARY RELATIONSHIPS

Indigenous missionary movements have sprung up. Karens from Burma have done considerable missionary work in northern Thailand for several generations. The first Thai missionary, however, went to Sarawak under the auspices of the Church of Christ in Thailand only three years ago.

The concept of "foreign missions" dies slowly in Thailand. For each missionary or fraternal worker who enters the country at the invitation of the Church of Christ in Thailand, to work in intimate partnership with it under its boards and agencies, a dozen "foreign missionaries" enter the country. These missionaries are answerable to a distant board in a far nation, responsible to no indigenous Thai group, and all too often they are moving in the intellectual and spiritual atmosphere of the nineteenth century. A new day demands a new interpretation of mission. The new nations of the world deserve something better than they have been receiving. The overseas worker has much to contribute to the Thai church, whether he comes from India, Korea, Japan, Indonesia, the Philippines or the United States. But the relationship must be one of equality, partnership in mission. The patronizing superiority of unilateral missionary endeavor strikes a note completely at odds with rising national consciousness, developing responsibility and mature churchmanship.

During the postwar era, for example, the Church of Christ in Thailand gradually took over from its mentor, the American Presbyterian Mission, its various functions until in August, 1957, the Thai church assumed full responsibility for the mission's five hospitals, its 20 schools and its 119 churches. A Presbyterian Church or mission no longer exists in Thailand. All cooperating churches have not yet actually merged with the Thai church, and many groups still remain outside. Largest of the independent bodies is the Roman Catholic Church. Today there are more than 100,000 Roman Catholics in Thailand, three times as many as the number of Protestants.

Cooperation with the Roman Catholics began before Vatican II and continues to grow. With the arrival of the Jesuits in 1954, some conversations between them and Thai Protestant churchmen began to take place. When it came time to open new university work in the provincial capital of Chiangmai, the two groups worked in the closest harmony and attempted actually to establish a joint project. Draft papers were prepared. Possible problems were anticipated. The time was not ripe then for a joint university project, but separate work still continues along lines of closest possible cooperation. From this experience grew others, and a Jesuit priest is now teaching in the Thailand Theological Seminary (Protestant). A Thai Bible for use both by Protestants and Catholics is being prepared. Cooperation in social work projects continues to expand. The Student Christian Movement meets regularly now with Catholic students, and Christian university professors do not meet except jointly. This adds up to a significant and dramatic new dimension to Christian mission in Thailand.

OLD WAYS AND NEW DAYS

The next largest groups outside the united church is the Overseas Missionary Fellowship, formerly known as the China Inland Mission. This group, which entered Thailand only after World War II, with resources transferred from

China, now numbers almost 200 missionaries. Perhaps because of its brief history, and also because much of its work is among the minority ethnic groups, it still claims a rather limited Thai constituency. The next two largest groups operating outside the united Protestant Church of Christ in Thailand are: the Christian and Missionary Alliance, which began its work in 1929 and now has more than 70 missionaries in the country and is especially known for its extensive work among lepers; and the Southern Baptists, who came after World War II and now have about 40 missionaries at work. There are also Seventh Day Adventists, Jehovah's Witnesses and other sects representing various shades of Pentecostalism and fundamentalism. To complicate the picture even further, there is an American Church of Christ Mission to Thailand and the Texas Church of Christ, in addition to the united Protestant "Church of Christ in Thailand." Disservice to the Christian cause comes with the introduction of schismatic, squabbling, pretentious denominationalism. The continuity and clarity of the Christian witness is compromised and obscured at precisely that historical moment when a clear and united voice is most needed. For other voices clamor for the attention of the Thai.

Air travel in recent years has made Bangkok the crossroads of Southeast Asia. It has become headquarters for various regional development and defense projects. It was chosen by the United Nations as headquarters in Southeast Asia for seven of its agencies, largest among them the Economic Commission for Asia and the Far East (ECAFE). Inevitably, Bangkok has found itself at the crossroads of the ecumenical movement too, and several major assemblies of the East Asia Christian Conference have met there. Out of more than 200 missionaries operating from one Asian church to another within the membership of the EACC, more than a dozen of them are in Thailand. Thus the Christian church tries to speak with a single voice, above the babble of competing denominations, but with a Southeast Asian inflection.

RURAL AND URBAN CHALLENGES

Ecumenical Christianity tries to make its presence felt in very practical ways. Its first concrete expression in Thailand took the form of a work camp in 1949, when young people assembled to repair wartime damage to the oldest Protestant church. The following year students from seven nations went to a new cooperative farm site in Chiangrai province to lay the foundations for a new church.

This farm itself symbolizes the role of the church in a new age. Sixty families, on a homesteading basis, with joint use of equipment and facilities, have created a center of agricultural influence in northern Thailand. Massive aid programs and government welfare services sometimes overshadow church efforts, but the church has an advantage, too. It is free from ulterior political purposes, free from massive governmental bureaucracy, free to experiment around the edges of a society and a culture. Such experimentation, as in this instance, may produce projects so vital that they indicate new directions for others. The continuing witness of the church can be dynamic. It can seek change rather than shun it. The Thai church is a rural church, and change must ultimately be felt in rural areas. It is a rice-farming church. In its rural program, the church encourages farmers to diversify their crops. For centuries rice farmers have spent half the year just waiting, waiting for the rains to come. Other crops could be grown during this period. Seeds could be provided and animal stock developed for improving strains. The agricultural church worker, and even more important, his Thai colleagues, can draw farmers together to plan, teach, train. Cooperative loan funds, cottage industries and crafts, may break the hold of money lenders and help to provide a strong economic base for a rural church. The church calls this its Rural Life and Rural Development Program. The church moves ahead.

While most of the Christians, and 80 percent of the population, live in the country, the future of Thailand is being determined at its very heart, the capital at Bangkok. There the various aid programs, the international agencies, the government bureaus, weld, forge and hammer out the programs and policies that will determine the development of this nation for decades and generations to come. A church that cannot find a voice at this power center is a peripheral church. A church that is to have any place whatsoever in the future must be articulate at those points in the culture where change is first conceived. In any society, the university tends to become a crucial center of change. Newspapers report the overthrow of governments by student action. Such direct political involvement is strange to Thailand; yet the people who will call the changes in the future are university students today. Here is a point at which the Christian church must find its voice.

The earliest approaches of the church to the university consisted almost entirely of "student work," that is, programs and activities for students. Many of these still continue. Shortly after the end of World War II the church requested a new study of its approach to the university.

This led to the establishment of a Student Christian Center in Bangkok. There were no universities outside of Bangkok then. This center provided badly needed residential facilities for men and women. More than that, it attempted to find a legitimate role for the church at the level of higher education by filling some of the functions of student unions or foundations in the United States. This included lectures, discussion groups, Bible study, worship, counseling and even some successful attempts to encourage the fine arts through drama, music and art. The church was moving from "student work" to actual involvement in the life and needs of the university and its community. Student center staff members lectured in the universities. Student center lecterns became forums for ideas and discussions that could find no place on campus, and the annual "seminars" became a matter of some importance and controversy. Through a combination of on-campus and off-campus emphases it proved to be a center for inquiry and experimentation. Now there are six fraternal workers or missionaries teaching with the universities, three Jesuit priests, and a few dozen Christian professors where two decades ago there were none.

This advance of the ministry of the church into and within the secular world of the university was strengthened by the development of a Student Christian Movement. Under a General Secretary recruited from Japan by the East Asia Christian Conference, SCM chapters have opened on each of the university campuses. With a membership now approaching 300, they concentrate quite heavily on the life and problems of the Christian in the university and have provided inspiring and educational retreats and conferences.

THE CHURCH AND SOCIETY

Penetration of the secular world has not been confined to the universities. There have been Christian ministers and young seminarians working in factories, and there are Christian social workers in the Department of Public Welfare. The dividing line between professional church worker and involved layman becomes increasingly hard to find.

Another focus of the church as it moves into the world of education is its seminary. Founded in 1886, reestablished in 1912 and again in 1948 in the northern city of Chiangmai, it has gone through a period of rapid change and growth as it has adjusted to the demands of a new church and a new day. It still devotes its major effort to training ministers for a rural church but also has departments of music, courses for laymen and different levels of study for students of varying backgrounds. The seminary has attempted to meet the problems of urbanization by a "semester-in-Bangkok" program, in which students go into residence in the university center and pursue an urban-oriented curriculum.

These two focuses, the Student Christian Center and the Thailand Theological Seminary, merge in the development of a new "Religion and Society" program, which promises to be the next major step in the church's continuing efforts to explore new patterns of ministry to the society in which it finds itself. A church need not always be immediately and directly involved in the power play within a society. It may be enough to be involved in the lives of those who make the determinative decisions. So, building upon its successes in the seminary and center, the church moves into an effort to provide a meeting place for the various religions, the community leaders and the Thai intelligentsia: A competent staff will encourage Buddhist-Christian dialogue, an adequate library will encourage interreligious study and research, and university professors will be drawn in for interdisciplinary exchange of ideas. Special extended seminars for laymen will attempt to bring them into a continuing conversation with the intellectual and religious communities. Pastor institutes will enable seminary graduates and older men to hear what others are thinking in different fields of work and study. Much of the Church and Labor program that has been developing in recent years may find its most effective and most far-reaching expression within this group.

NEW LEADERSHIP FOR A NEW ERA

But new plans presuppose Thai leadership. The church knows that leadership training must come before all else. Since the end of World War II it has provided a total of more than 1,000 years of scholarship study at home and abroad for its young people. Because education is the only door to a useful future, many parents will sacrifice all to provide education for their children. Compulsory education extends through the seventh grade. Government schools or church schools with low tuition carry them through to college. Even at the university level, a student may secure a year of education for less than $300—but even this is a lot of money on an annual income of $600.

During this postwar period more than 100 Christian students have been provided with scholarships for university education within Thailand, and almost as many have had an opportunity to pursue graduate study abroad. This means that the Thai society, its universities, businesses and bureaucracy, is being fed a thin but continuing stream of able young Christians. Not only that, but church-related hospitals are being supplied with well-trained doctors and nurses, and young teachers, many with advanced degrees, are flowing into the church schools.

Typical of the new leadership produced by this program is Koson Srisang, a boy from a remote village in the northeast. In a tiny rural school in the farthest rice paddies of a depressed district, a teacher saw signs of promise in the little boy and urged him to take a Fulbright test. One of the schools acceptable for Fulbright grants was Prince Royal's College, a church school, where he became a Christian. Like most new Christians, he took his faith seriously and was actively involved in the Student Christian Movement in that school. He went on to Bangkok and the university with a church scholarship, and he studied to become a teacher. He was also president of his class and a leader in his school activities. After his graduation, again through Fulbright scholarship funds, he went to the University of Minnesota for his Master's degree, returning to take up responsibilities in the literature and literacy program of the church. He was called to assume the directorship of the Student Christian Center, where he performed brilliantly, bringing church, university and community into closer communication than ever before. Then again under a church scholarship, Koson went to America, where he is now studying for a doctorate in theology and sociology in preparation for a life of service to his church and nation. He has earned the support which the church has been able to give him. As with many others, his own devotion, loyalty and competence make possible a successful program of leadership development.

A VENERABLE FAITH

The church in Thailand speaks in and to a Buddhist land. This fact at once renders comparisons with churches in other lands almost impossible. Buddhism, the state religion of Thailand, has been defined as "that religion which without beginning with God leads man to the place where God is not necessary." The Theravada form, sometimes called Southern Buddhism, prevails in Thailand as in Burma, Cambodia, Laos and Ceylon. Is it growing stronger or weaker in Thailand? Surely nationalism is on the increase, and Buddhism is the handmaiden of nationalism in Thailand. Buddhism, however, is a passive, tolerant religion. There have been only two outbursts of persecution against Christianity in the several centuries of Christian presence, both of these under somewhat extenuating circumstances. But while tolerant, Buddhism is unbending; while serene, it is unyielding.

It took 20 years to win the first Thai Protestant convert more than a century ago. It is still easier to win converts among animists in the north than among Buddhists in the south. A hasty glance at Buddhism provides a clue to why there are few converts. The Buddhist religion fosters noninvolvement, noncommitment. A Buddhist tends to avoid taking a "stand" if he can. The confession of faith required by the Christian religion is a form of open commitment from which the Buddhist almost instinctively recoils.

According to tradition, Buddhist belief and doctrine come directly from Buddha himself, whose 2500th birthday was celebrated a few years ago. The Buddhism that came to Thailand from India and Ceylon at the beginning of the

Christian era attributes all suffering to desire. A good Buddhist therefore tries to suppress all desire. This curbs suffering, which is a result of desire, and also advantageously influences the cycle of rebirth. The "go-go-go" attitudes of the West find no congenial home in the Buddhist bosom.

Buddha was a teacher. While many miracles and wonders are ascribed to him, he is not actually to be worshiped as a god. Worship, rather, is more a matter of paying respect by lighting candles and offering gifts to priests. All acts of respect and obeisance produce "merit" for the participant. Merit is also gained by obeying the code of ethics, as set forth in the Eight-fold Path, and by suppressing all desire. The merit gained affects rebirth and reincarnation. The Eight-fold Path consists of Right Understanding, Right Purpose, Right Speech, Right Action, Right Livelihood, Right Effort, Right Mindfulness, and Right Concentration. Three basic principles underlie this ethical system: 1) all matter is transitory, 2) life consists of suffering and 3) the soul itself is but an illusion. One's good deeds (and bad) are totaled to determine one's *kharma,* or reward and punishment. Do good and you will be rewarded; do evil and you will be punished.

If Christianity can be called the "religion of the agonized conscience," Buddhism might be tagged the "religion of proper behavior," for as long as one follows the Eight-fold Path, behaves well, there is nothing to fear. Thus Christianity has tended to produce what some have called an "inner-directed" or "guilt" culture, while Buddhism has tended to produce what has been called too simply an "other-directed" or "shame" culture. In very practical terms this means that the Thai culture has tended to be authoritative, almost feudal in its social patterns, with more emphasis placed on obedience than on initiative, a higher value placed upon form than upon content. Tradition thus rates more highly as a virtue than do curiosity, novelty, experimentation. Passivity is preferable to rebellion. Memory serves one better in the university than does individual research or self-expression. Respect for one's superiors or one's betters is the oil that smooths the operation of the social machinery. Such glib generalities about a culture are dangerous and never wholly true, but they may provide a flash of insight for the outsider into cultural contrasts and differences.

Comparisons between Buddhism and Christianity indicate many similarities. Even a cursory glance at the Eightfold Path suggests parallels with the Ten Commandments. Both religions have developed groups of monks who wear robes, albeit different colors, and shave their heads. Both have what they call a Lenten season. A miraculous birth is attributed to both Buddha and Jesus, and both are said to have been worshiped by a wise man or men led by a star. Miracles and halos are attributed to both men, and groups of their disciples established churches and missionary programs. Both religions have filled their places of worship with holy objects, statues and bric-a-brac. But despite such superficial similarities, there is a vast difference in world view.

The Buddhist, with his cyclical interpretation of history, the endless repetition of life and death, and cycles of rebirth and reincarnation, is in startling contrast to the Christian with his viewpoint of God as Alpha and Omega, the beginning and the end, and his lineal concept of history that sweeps men and nations along in a continuous line. God as Lord of history, the architect of events both for men and for nations, offers a different world indeed from the Buddhist's *kharma* or fate. The Christian doctrine of the grace of God finds no counterpart in Buddhism. If one's fate is determined by one's deeds, the concept of the grace of God has no meaning. The argument is not too different from that of the relative efficacy of faith and works in determining man's salvation.

This is too short a description of the environment within which the Christian church works in Thailand. Buddhism and Christianity have lived in friendly association with each other most of the time. Christianity may have performed one of its greatest services by stimulating Buddhism to self-examination and adaptation. For better or for worse, for good or for evil, Christianity was partner to the introduction of Western civilization. With its hospitals and its schools, there came an element of compassion for the needs of people, their problems, their social welfare. Over the last century Buddhist governments have consistently taken on these concerns as their own.

At assemblies of social welfare workers it is usually the custom to open proceedings with an address by a high government official, who speaks first of the historic role of Buddhism in ministering to the needs of the people. He may use Buddhist scriptural references to illustrate and justify this concern. Rather than feeling sensitive at not having received credit for its stimulating role in this process, the Christian church should take pride in the adoption and adaptation process that has run so smoothly. The Christian contribution to the advance and progress of a nation or a society need not always be flaunted for all to see. Credit is cheap reward for service well rendered.

What then does the phrase "resurgence of non-Christian

religions" mean in Thailand? Is Buddhism actually a resurgent religion? To the extent to which it embodies nationalistic and provincial aspirations, it may be. To the extent to which it is being "used" by political forces as a part of an anti-Communist campaign, it surely is. To the extent to which Buddhism can supply the necessary emotional pressure to stir up strains of nationalism, to that extent, too, it is resurgent. As a motivating force in the daily lives of people, however, it does not look resurgent.

The Buddist temple used to be the center of the life of the village. But today, hotels have robbed it of its function as a hostel for travelers; public schools are stripping it of its role as the primary agent for education; and government hospitals have completely taken over the temple's ministry to the ill in body and mind. National military conscription has played havoc with the ancient tradition calling on young men to enter the priesthood. The Department of Public Welfare has effectively taken over the temple's ministry to the indigent and the cast-offs, the orphans and the foundlings. Under the battering impact of Western culture and the twentieth century, the functional roles played by Buddhism in Thai society have thus slipped over to the central bureaucracy. What becomes of a religion thus stripped of its functional role? The same question hangs heavy over the West. Secularized society functions without reference to its religious antecedents. The Thai university world is probably almost as thoroughly secularized as is the university world in the West.

The secularizing process may have stripped Buddhism of its function, but certainly not of its forms. Nominal Buddhism, with its ceremonies of homage within the classroom, government and university offices, is never challenged or questioned. To do so would be an unthinkable breach of patriotism and etiquette. The forms are not about to be surrendered, for they are so deeply ingrained in the Thai habit pattern that they constitute almost reflexive reactions. The day may possibly come when the forms are rejected by a new generation much as they have been rejected in the Christian West, but there is no sign of it yet. The loyalty to Buddhist rites and ceremonies is intense and unquestioning. And hollow.

How important are the "forms" in which a religion is wrapped? There are those who believe that Christianity in Asia may have been too slow in picking up and adapting Asian form and ceremony to Christian belief and theology. The Thai wedding, for example, involves a lovely ceremony of pouring water over the hands of bride and groom from a conch shell as they kneel side by side, their heads bound together by a jasmine loop. There is little in this that could not adequately symbolize Christian marriage. In contrast, however, Buddhist temple architecture presents problems, for many of its symbols recall Buddhist faith and practice in such ways as to make Christians recoil.

Buddhism, with the king at its head, has long supplied a large measure of stability to the Thai society. It has tended to preserve what is good from the past, while Christianity has provided something of that other necessary function in any culture, the stimulation of creative change. The greatest contribution of Christianity to Thailand is not to be measured in numbers of converts but in the extent to which it has stimulated a society in profound need of change to face and meet the demands of the twentieth century.

Confronted with a period of rapid or revolutionary change, a religion may do one of two things. It may fall back upon its forms, its outward practices, in which case it is almost surely doomed to extinction or at best irrelevance. Or it may search its own Scriptures and its own past for the resources with which to confront the future.

A formalized religion tends to associate itself with a particular form of government or ideology, for example, democracy or monarchy, capitalism or socialism. Such a religion runs the risk of the dinosaur, ultimate extinction, as the system to which it ties itself fades into the past. This is true of both Christianity and Buddhism. During this period of upset and change, Christianity occupies a strong position from which to continue its historic function as stimulant to the Thai society, for it is not yet tied to the Thai society or culture. Contemporary change in Thailand focuses sharply on modifying the patterns of externally applied authority. Christianity has much to offer from its own faith and its own history, most especially the high value it places on the worth of each individual before God, the equality of all his children, the direct relationship between the individual and God. Christianity moves with the tide, for it moves toward the future.

WHAT FUTURE?

With Thailand packed from north to south with foreign advisors, AID programs, United Nations agencies, capital investment schemes, Peace Corps and other volunteer programs, an indigenous Thai Christian church has a unique and important role to play, that of continuity of witness. The church has no monopoly on dedicated service or on competence and ability. But from within the Thai culture itself, it is now able to provide a continuing witness to the gospel. This builds up, year after year, to a cumulative impact far exceeding its statistical growth. Workers in other agencies come and go. One- and two-year assignments allow little time for learning a language and absorbing a culture. The Christian worker has something different to offer: continuous and loyal service. He stays, for it is his church. It may even be true that a less brilliant worker, staying for a longer period of time, carries proportionately greater influence in a society that cherishes relationships more than accomplishments, seniority more than brilliance. This the Christian church has provided over the centuries and the years—identification in the growth of a nation, and in its progressive movement into and through the twentieth century. This its workers have been able to bring to it—identification that bespeaks permanence of relationship.

The church in Thailand, in the northern reaches of the kingdom, in its rice paddies and jungles, in its teeming streets and crowded rivers, and the church beyond the seas, are all involved in the tedious task of nation building. They share the knowledge of a God of history who guides the destinies of men and nations, a God so closely related to each and every living soul that he gave his Son for them. This the Christian church proclaims, to a world in turmoil, to its men, to its nations.

3 VIETNAM CAMBODIA and LAOS

the church at the crossroads of chaos

René De Roeck*

VIETNAM, CAMBODIA and Laos form an arc-shaped bloc that fills the southeastern tip of mainland Asia. Sharing a common history of French domination, the countries today are separate political entities: North Vietnam a "democratic republic," South Vietnam an "independent republic," while both Cambodia and Laos have the status of independent kingdoms.

VIETNAM

The People

Thirty-four million people live in this war-torn and divided country. The southern frontier is nearly 1,500 miles

* Translated by Stephen Neill.

from the northern; the breadth of the country varies between 40 and 250 miles. The most important ethnic group are the Viets, who are to be found in every part of the country. Nearly two million Chinese, mostly resident in the towns, make up another part of the population. The majority of the Chinese are Vietnamese citizens, but they retain their own language and customs and have made for themselves a separate place within the life of the nation—a situation that gives rise to a variety of problems.

The high plateaus of central Vietnam are the home of a number of primitive tribes, all that are left of the original inhabitants of this area, who were driven into the hills some centuries ago by pressure from the Viets. They number about half a million. In spite of the differences in origin, language and civilization among these tribes, they are commonly grouped together as "mountain peoples."

Finally, in the south we find an important minority (perhaps 300,000) of Khmer origin.

Vietnam lives for the most part from the produce of the soil—rice, fruit, rubber, tea, coffee.

Traditional Beliefs

The traditional religion of the Viets is a mixture of Mahayana Buddhism and Taoism (within which are to be found traces of ancestor worship and Confucian morality). The most important factor is actually ancestor worship, a worship that has inspired filial piety, respect for others and devotion. This form of worship has exercised a profoundly civilizing influence, and in the course of centuries has fashioned Vietnamese society, which is steeped in Chinese humanism and the doctrine of Confucius.

Thirty years ago there came into existence a new religion

vhich is genuinely Vietnamese—Caodaism. This is a syn-
retistic system, combining with a rather ill-defined belief
n a supreme God (Cao-Dai, the Most High) elements
lrawn from other Oriental religions and from Christianity.
3etween 1945 and 1955 certain political decisions taken by
he leaders of this group brought about dissension and di-
risions, marring the harmony and brotherly spirit they had
lreamed of producing. At the present time the number of
dherents of Caodai is nearly two million.

Another indigenous sect is Hoa-Hao, which has several
housand adherents concentrated in the western provinces
f the South.

In recent years there has been a revival of Buddhism in
Vietnam, as elsewhere in Asia. Here, however, the revival
vas in large part a reaction against the pressure exercised
rom without by Roman Catholicism, an influence that be-
:ame increasingly aggressive under the regime of Ngo
Dinh Diem. Buddhist secondary schools and orphanages
vere brought into being; social services were undertaken;
ind great public celebrations were organized on the occa-
ion of each religious festival. Apparently, up to the present
ime much of this activity has been used mainly for political
ourposes. It will be necessary to wait some time before
ittempting to judge its religious significance.

On the coast of central Vietnam, in the plain of Phan
Rang, live the Chams who, long ago before the arrival of
he Viets, ruled this entire region (they were at the height
f their power in about the sixth century). They number
:5,000, of whom 80 percent are Muslims. For centuries
hey have maintained contact, along the sea routes, with
heir brethren in Indonesia.

It would be difficult to report here in detail on the beliefs of the various tribes of the mountain peoples. It is possible however, to say that they can all be grouped under the general heading of animist.

The Roman Catholic Mission

Roman Catholic missionary work in Vietnam began i earnest in the sixteenth century, though there are traces o activity as early as the fourteenth century. By the middle o the seventeenth century, there were 300,000 baptized per sons. It was at this time that Father Alexander de Rhode began to transliterate into Latin characters the words of th Vietnamese language, which until that time had alway been written in Chinese characters. His transliteration i still in use today. The first catechism in Latin-Vietnames was printed a few years later and provided the missionarie with an indispensable tool for their work. The history o Catholic work until the end of the nineteenth century wa marked by episodes of exile and martyrdom (in 1851, dur ing the most severe persecution, at least 117 priests an 90,000 Christians perished), but the preaching of the gospe continued despite adversity. In 1933 the first Vietnames bishop was consecrated, thus marking "the beginning o the end" of the missionary period. This development, how ever, has been affected by the war for independence, wit its accompanying miseries. As a result of the Geneva Agree ment in 1954, 800,000 persons, three-quarters of whom wer Christians, moved from North to South Vietnam.[1]

[1] The Geneva Agreement of 1954, agreed to by all except the Unite States, provided for a provisional partition of the territory of Vietnam the North remaining in the hands of the Vietminh, a revolutionar group of Communist allegiance, and the South controlled by th Nationalist regime. An interim period of several months was pro

North Vietnam did its utmost, though without marked iccess, to bring the church under its control and to transrm it into a national church separated from Rome and ibservient to the state. All the foreign missionaries were ompelled, on one pretext or another, to leave the country. he last, a French Dominican, Fr. Léna, left in 1960.

South Vietnam adopted a constitution that guarantees eligious freedom. But the continuing military conflict has revented the emergence of a stable political and religious ituation. As a consequence, the people tend to turn to the ld traditional powers—Buddhism, the church and in some egree the army. This has produced a grave confusion of eligion and politics and is a serious source of weakness to he nation. Many are discontented, many are undecided, nd it has proved impossible to build up a common front gainst the enemy without and within.

The Roman Catholic Church Today

The *Catholic Annual of Vietnam*, the last issue of which ppeared in 1964, reported that in North Vietnam there vere 833,000 Roman Catholics, with 10 bishops and 361 riests; whereas in South Vietnam there were 1,430,000 Catholics, 13 bishops (twelve Vietnamese, one foreigner) nd 1,227 priests (among them 160 foreign missionaries).

The striking fact about these figures relating to the outh is the large number of Vietnamese bishops and riests. In contrast to most of the other countries in which nissions are at work, in Vietnam the indigenous element is

ided in order to make it possible for citizens who wished to do so o cross the frontier in one direction or the other. Actually this esulted in a terrible loss of face for the Communist North, as a eritable exodus from North to South followed.

not only in the majority, but the Vietnamese Catholics a
in fact masters in their own ecclesiastical house. This fa
is of the utmost importance for the future development
the church. Roman Catholics are to be found on all soci
levels, as much among the humble peasants of the ri
fields as among the higher ranks of the civil officials. The
are also a number of sympathizers who have not been ba
tized—former students in mission schools, former membe
of the Christian youth movement.

In the light of all these facts, we can say that the churc
has really taken root in Vietnam. Certainly it will nee
missionaries for some time to come, but from now on th
Vietnamese will determine the destiny of their own churc
It must be admitted, however, that this church is still e
tremely Western in its thought forms and outward appea
ance. But new possibilities are now open to the church i
Vietnam, thanks to the existence of a Christian elite, bot
lay and ordained, and the church must rethink Christ an
his gospel in such a fashion as to present them in a manne
adapted to the needs of the people of Vietnam.

In such a church, the role of the missionary is clearl
that of a helper. All missionary work today is carried ou
under the direction of the Vietnamese bishops or in th
closest collaboration with them. An indigenous episcopat
forms a normal part of the evangelization of the country
it is the sign of maturity of the church. Today the mission
ary puts himself at the disposal of the national church
which makes use of him according to his qualifications an
interests. Fifteen nations are represented among the 16
Catholic foreign missionaries now resident in South Viet
nam.

The lay people admirably support the work of the clergy

Already for a considerable period they have been responsible for the organization of the parishes and the various associations. Therefore, Christian life can go on even if the priest has had to leave or if there are certain areas which he is able to visit only rarely.

In a country devastated by an ever-expanding struggle, which has produced the disastrous results with which we are all familiar, there is a mass of urgent and immediate problems. As a result, some problems of more general significance do not receive the attention that is their due, not so much from the authorities of the church as from the general run of the faithful. One of these problems is ecumenism. In Saigon there has been for a number of years the joy of ecumenical encounters, especially in connection with the week of prayer for unity. The Roman Catholic Archbishop himself has on occasion gone out of his way to be present at such joint meetings for prayer and meditation. The Second Vatican Council, and the extensive rethinking to which it has given rise, have undoubtedly had a favorable influence on such meetings. The number of those taking part in them has always been small, however, and the Protestants have been represented almost exclusively by members of the Reformed Church of France. The other confessions, which mostly belong to or have grown out of the Christian and Missionary Alliance, will have nothing to do with these attempts at fellowship, which ought to draw together all those who have accepted the gospel of Jesus Christ. Outside of Saigon, with a few exceptions, everyone lives in complete ignorance of who the others are and what they are doing.

In North Vietnam, a considerable community of Christians still exists. It is not difficult to imagine the problems with which they have to wrestle in this republic. Press, schools, youth movements have disappeared or have been nationalized. The small number of priests is also a great handicap, especially because the authorities do their utmost to hinder their movements. Young people are compelled to join associations of "pioneers," which means that they become less accessible to the authority and influence of their parents and teachers. The authorities are prepared to tolerate the existence of the church, provided that it is national —that is, independent of Rome. (It was impossible for the bishops here to go to Rome to attend the Second Vatican Council.) Furthermore, the church must become a docile instrument in the hands of the state; hence the attempt to bring into being a movement of "patriotic priests," who, without being formally pledged to the services of the state, will come to be zealous supporters of state programs.

To read the decree on religious questions (1955) makes one aware of the spirit that guides the rulers of North Vietnam. First of all, religious liberty is declared, together with the right of the priests to preach in church (and, in consequence, nowhere else!). The state reserves the right to prescribe to the priests the subjects on which they are to preach: "While preaching religion, the ministers of the various cults are also under the obligation to inculcate into the minds of the faithful patriotism, the sense of their civic duties, respect for the democratic authorities and for the people's Republic" (Article 1, para. 3). The decree is careful to announce the principles which, in given cases, can (as in China) be used as a pretext for action against the clergy and the believers: "The law will take penal action against anyone, who under pretext of religion shall attack peace, unity, independence and democracy, shall engage in propaganda on behalf of war, or shall attack the liberty or the ideas of any other person."

Under such conditions, it is scarcely possible to hope that the church will be able to grow. Happily, however, the rare pieces of news that come from the other side of the bamboo curtain indicate that the life of the church continues to be maintained and may even be growing in strength, for Christians are driven to take a stand. Nonetheless, the heavy hand of the state, resting on the youth, makes prospects for the future rather gloomy.

Protestant Mission History

Only at the beginning of the twentieth century was Protestant interest in missionary work in Vietnam directly awakened, when the Christian and Missionary Alliance (CMA) took Indochina as one of its fields of missionary operation. The first approaches were frustrated by mistrust on the part of the French authorities, and it was not until 1911 that the CMA received permission to establish its first station in Vietnam. In that year three of their missionaries from South China, including Dr. R. A. Jaffray, took up residence at Tourane (now Danang). Four years later, missionaries found their way to Haiphong and later to Hanoi. The mission at Hanoi developed rapidly, and it was not long before the missionaries were able to produce a translation of the Bible into the Vietnamese language. A few years later the mission extended its operations to the South, principally to Saigon and Mytho, but made slow progress in this area as a result of endless difficulties with minor officials of the French colonial government. When Dr. Alfred C. Snead, General Secretary of the CMA, visited Vietnam in 1927, he found 5,000 Evangelical Christians organized in small, living communities, in most cases under the direction of a Vietnamese pastor.

The rapid expansion of Protestant work in Vietnam is closely linked to the excellent work carried out by the Bible School at Tourane, and to the groups of indigenous workers that it was able to turn out in a remarkably short time. The Vietnamese were to be evangelized by Vietnamese. This school, founded in 1921, grew of course from small beginnings, but by 1927 the first Vietnamese graduates were ready to go out into the work of the mission. In that same year, a general meeting of the church was held at Tourane. Certainly the most important decision taken at this time was the formation of the Evangelical Church of Vietnam, a self-supporting national church. From then on the mission to Vietnam was to be primarily the responsibility of the Vietnamese themselves, with the missionaries more and more in the background as fraternal advisors, inspirers of others.

Through the Japanese occupation and later the war of Independence, the missionaries were first reduced to inaction and then the greater part of them were compelled to leave. The year 1945 was one of particular hardship, and the faith of believers was subjected to severe tests. The misery of the time, the excitements and excesses of intense nationalism and endless pressures, were in some cases too much for the faith of Christians, and led to a number of defections. Others paid for fidelity with their lives.

From 1946 onward, the Vietnamese pastors were again able to move about. Their first task was to seek out the believers who still remained, in order to regroup them and bring the scattered communities back to life. In 1965 the CMA reported the following figures for the Evangelical

Church in Vietnam (the South only): 41,700 baptized adults and 18,600 inquirers, of whom a considerable number are refugees from the North, in 335 churches, cared for by 412 national workers, of whom 104 are ordained, and 30 CMA missionaries. The total Evangelical constituency in the South in 1967 was estimated at 150,000.

Protestant Missions Today

The Evangelical Church in Vietnam, related to the CMA, continues its active missionary work in all the various areas of free Vietnam. The greater flexibility introduced by Diem's government into the laws controlling the purchase of land (1956–57) has made it possible to put up a number of new places of worship, and this increased visible presence of the church has had an excellent effect.

In 1960 the Bible School of Tourane (Danang) was moved to Nha Trang, a port situated about 300 miles north of Saigon. Young people who have completed their studies in secondary school come here for three years of training in biblical studies before going out into the work of the Christian ministry. A six-month course is provided for those who wish to work as catechists under the guidance of the pastors.

Danang, the cradle of Protestantism in Vietnam, continues to be a very active missionary center. The Evangelical Church has four congregations with 1,600 members; the Seventh Day Adventists, the Southern Baptists, and the Church of Christ all have work here. In addition, the Worldwide Evangelization Crusade has at Danang an orphanage with 80 children, and a leper asylum with 180 patients. In all, seven missionaries, including a doctor and two nurses, along with 30 Vietnamese evangelists, care for a number of Christian communities in Danang, the membership of which is reckoned to be between 6,000 and 8,000.

Dalat, a hill station about 180 miles north of Saigon, was an active center of missionary work even before the war. Dalat was the starting point of the movement for the evangelization of the tribes of mountain people. Here are to be found the language school for missionaries, a rest home, a Bible school that yearly trains 30 evangelists for the mountain people, a small hospital and a primary school for the children of the tribal people. A press, which had been in operation there since 1954, has now been transferred to Saigon. There was a school and a boarding home for the children of missionaries, but the increasing insecurity has led the heads of the mission to transfer the entire institution to Bangkok. We must mention also the extensive work of translation into the various dialects of the mountain people carried on in this center. Furthermore, there is CMA and Adventist work in the communities of Di Linh, Dran and Fyan, as well as the parish and the leper asylum of the CMA at Banmethuot.

In 1957 the first preachers from among the mountain people were ordained. The Gospels have been translated into Koho, Raday and Sre. The number of Christians among the mountain people is estimated at 10,000. Missionary work in these regions is rendered difficult by the long distances that have to be traveled and by the lack of roads. In addition, certain villages are always on the move, and groups of Vietcong guerrillas in this area do not look with favor on these movements. Sometimes travel brings acute danger; two missionaries were murdered on the road between Saigon and Dalat in 1963.

The majority of the Protestant missionaries are American. This may not be a serious drawback in relation to the majority of the Vietnamese, a hospitable and level-headed people; but it can become a grave handicap when the missionary is faced by embittered or excited people, or directly by the soldiers of the Vietcong.

In addition to the Protestant groups already mentioned, there is work carried on by Overseas Crusade, the Navigators, Overseas Missionary Fellowship, Wycliffe Bible Translators and World Vision. The Reformed Church of France has directed its attention mainly to French citizens and to those who can speak French. This may appear a rather narrow field, since it involves no direct missionary responsibility, but actually the influence of this church reaches out beyond its particular concerns. Now, in co-operation with the Evangelical Church of Vietnam, it has succeeded in opening in Saigon a kindergarten, a secondary school, a Bible school and a residence for students; and these are considered only a beginning. Saigon, of course, has become a center of missionary activity, a place where scholars, translators and administrators come together.

Of particular importance in Vietnam today is the special ministry of mercy and compassion carried on among the more than one million soul-sick and war-weary refugees. Since 1954 the Mennonites have pioneered in relief work in Vietnam. With the escalation of the war, however, other Protestant churches working through Church World Service, Lutheran World Relief and the Mennonite Central Committee have set up an agency called Vietnam Christian Service, to provide greater resources and services to those in need. With 69 Westerners working in VCS in 1967, the aim is to provide both relief and renewal of life. The work-

ers include doctors and nurses, agriculturists, home econ
omists, social workers, mechanics and teachers. They en
gage in public health education, community developmen
and handicraft programs, as well as direct ministries o
healing and relief. Additional relief work is carried on by
Asian Christian Service in Vietnam, an agency of the Eas
Asia Christian Conference. Increasingly there is concern fo
designing a major program of rehabilitation and reconstruc
tion of the country, which will be badly needed when peace
comes.

The misery and suffering in Vietnam compares to that in
Europe during and after World War II. It is almost im
possible to comprehend, let alone to describe. Steve Cary
member of a Quaker mission to Vietnam, spoke of it when
he reported:

> The people of Vietnam, after a quarter of a century of
> almost uninterrupted war in which they feel themselves to
> have no stake, see only the promise of worse to come.
> Both sides are now employing tactics that numb the soul.
> The agony of rural Vietnam where 75 per cent of the peo-
> ple live must be seen to be comprehended. It is found in
> the faces of widows and orphans, the hurt and the home-
> less, the harassed and the fearful, and their name is
> Legion.
>
> Although homelessness, hunger, and disease plague the
> people, it is the agony of incessant uncertainty which op-
> presses the population most. There is no front, and the
> front is everywhere.
>
> The village never knows in the morning if this will be
> the day when death comes from the air, and never knows
> at evening whether this will be the night death comes
> with stealth. Living in this situation produces a constant
> agony that is hard to describe.

Problems and Prospects

A number of urgent internal problems of missionary strategy and policy face the Protestant churches. For too long the work of preaching the gospel has been concerned only with the peasants and the lower middle class. There is a need to evangelize also the intellectual upper class, which can have greater influence in determining the tone and direction of affairs in the nation.

The genuine autonomy of the younger churches must become a reality. Some members of the younger churches complain that they are still in the process of "being hatched." This means that, where it has not already been done, the transfer of real authority to the younger churches must be accomplished.

Missionary methods also need to be reconsidered. It is not enough today to think simply in terms of the salvation of souls; the whole man needs to be redeemed and renewed. The message and action of Christ relates to man in his actual situation, man with his soul and his body. The fullness of the gospel message must be recovered.

All the servants of Christ should cooperate and carry out their programs of evangelization together; but the CMA, with its conservative theological orientation, has up to the present time shown little inclination toward cooperation.

When any ecumenical assembly of churches in Asia takes place, the Evangelical Church of Vietnam (together with those of Cambodia and Laos, which are also in large measure the fruit of CMA work) are always conspicuously absent. The American missionaries have taught the Vietnamese Protestants to be extremely cautious in relations with churches which do not share the conservative doc-

trinal position of the CMA. It is not difficult to understand why the Evangelical Church of Vietnam shows no
desire to have any relations of any kind whatever with the
Roman Catholic Church, when we see that the CMA is
not even prepared to cooperate with other Protestant
churches within the framework of the ecumenical movement.[2]

Fortunately, some Protestants do recognize the necessity
of ecumenical relationships in this new day, first between
the various Protestant confessions and then with the Roman
Catholic Church. It is their hope to be able to serve as
intermediaries, and then to bring about a greater measure
of unity. But so far there is little to record in the way of
results. For some years the Reformed Church of France
has joined with priests and laymen of the Roman Catholic
Church in meetings for prayer and meditation. These followers of Christ from separated traditions have prayed together and have learned to know one another better. Those
who have taken part in these meetings are anxious not
merely that they should be continued, but that the circle
of those taking part should be enlarged, drawing in members of other confessions. This is certainly a small ray of
hope for the future.

The war in Vietnam is making the mission of the
churches both more difficult and more imperative. Thousands of people in the South, harassed by forces from both
sides, are fleeing from their villages so as not to be caught
in the military crossfire. They crowd the larger villages and
towns where they must be housed, fed, nursed and con-
soled.

[2] Pierre Médard, "Catholiques et Protestants au Vietnam," *Eglise Vivante,* XI, No. 6 (1959), pp. 445–446.

Spiritually and intellectually, many Vietnamese no longer know who or where they are. They cannot think straight; they only want to be left alone. Ten years ago the refugee in Vietnam was a refugee from communism—an ideological refugee. Today, he may be a refugee from typhoon and flood, sometimes from communism, but mostly from war. He is not necessarily pro-Saigon, nor is he necessarily pro-Vietcong. It is estimated that there are three groups of people in South Vietnam today: 10 percent strongly pro-Communist; 10 percent strongly pro-Saigon; the other 80 percent noncommitted. The latter are people buffeted about by war for more than 25 years—disillusioned, cynical and having no real stake whatsoever in the outcome of this conflict. They feel they are pawns in a power struggle between great external powers, and they only wish the whole thing would end and that all foreigners would go home.

In the midst of this conflict a number of non-Christians have been impressed by the charity and concern of the Christian churches. They are attracted by the solidarity of the gospel and the great source of comfort it provides. Some of these non-Christians are thinking seriously about Jesus Christ, and possibly through saving faith in the Lord they will come to triumph over tragedy and find hope.

CAMBODIA

This country of about six million inhabitants consists of a vast plain, divided between forests and rice fields. About 90 percent of the people are Khmers, but there are also 350,000 Vietnamese, 250,000 Chinese, 85,000 Shans and, in the forests of the northeast, several thousand aborigines. Rice and fish are the principal resources, and industry is on the level of individual effort.

Beliefs

The greater part of the population is Buddhist. 75,000 monks live in nearly 3,000 monasteries; and the majority of the young people spend a period of their lives in training in a monastery, in many cases a year, sometimes more. Instruction in the Buddhist religion is obligatory in all schools. There are also about 100,000 Muslims, a religious community that came into being through contact with the Malays. Religious life among Muslims is active, and they support a number of schools.

The Roman Catholic Mission

The first missionary to visit Cambodia, Father F. Pinto, arrived in the middle of the sixteenth century. Attempts at preaching the gospel were made, and in 1576 the church in Cambodia was enriched by its first martyr, Father Sylvester de Azevedo. Work continued, but slowly, the difficulties being numerous. Only in 1770, as a result of the work of Father Levasseur, was the church provided with a translation of the catechism in the Khmer language—and in spite of this accomplishment, no progress was made. When Monsignor Miche arrived in 1842, he found only four churches and 250 baptized Christians.

At the present time the Roman Catholic Church has one bishop (a French missionary) and 57 priests—about 40 French, 15 Vietnamese and two or three Khmers—who have under their care 54,000 Catholics, the greater part of whom are Vietnamese. The trouble is that there are hardly as many as 2,000 Catholics of the Khmer race, a handful of Chinese, and all the others are Vietnamese. Once again the church takes on the appearance of an imported article, intended only for the use of foreigners. Worse still, it gives the impression of being Vietnamese, and it was the Vietnamese who gradually drove the Khmers out of what is now South Vietnam. In consequence, they are hereditary enemies and the difficulties, far from growing less, are growing worse all the time. As a result of uncertainty about exactly where the frontier runs, violent incidents are numerous, and it seems unlikely that peaceful relationships will be restored in the near future.

Instruction in the Khmer language has been made obligatory in all schools; in consequence, all the bush schools (and that means Christian schools), which were teaching in the Vietnamese language, have had to be closed.

Without being actually hostile to the missions, the government imposes restrictions on the entry of foreign missionaries. Only in 1957 was it possible to proceed with the ordination of the first Khmer priest.

Protestant Missions

The king had always refused permission for the entry of Protestant missionaries, as long as the French authorities remained neutral. In 1922, however, the CMA sent out a missionary family, which managed to take up residence in Phnom Penh, and a year later a second, which was successful in taking up residence in Battambang. Beginnings were on a very modest scale. There was first the difficulty of learning the Cambodian language, and until that was achieved, American missionaries had to communicate in French with the small number of Cambodians who had mastered that language. Extreme discretion was needed at all times in order not to attract the attention of the authorities.

In 1929, however, a small Bible school was opened. Its aim was to train future Cambodian preachers as soon as possible to a level that would equip them to carry the gospel to their brethren. In spite of great efforts, this mission developed only very slowly; first a few score, and then a few hundred believers. In 1965 the American missionaries were compelled to leave the country. Only one French couple is representing the CMA there today, and the work is, at best, in a "holding stage."

The problem for these missionaries has been to recognize the fact that the period of the "classic" missions is now at an end. More and more the younger churches have a feeling of their own independence, and they are no longer prepared to put up with the domination of a foreign mission, as they were in the past.

The Khmer Evangelical Church, brought into being by the work of the CMA, is now setting to work in the face of a considerable number of difficulties. The view of the government is that, since Buddhism is the state religion, any kind of preaching of the gospel is undesirable. The Constitution recognizes freedom of worship. This freedom, however, has not been fully maintained since the departure of the American missionaries, for the government of Cambodia was afraid that Protestant Cambodians might have come under political influences and no longer be loyal to it. Gradually the pressure has been relaxed, and at the present time Christians experience no difficulty in carrying on their worship. But prudence and discretion are still absolutely necessary. There can be no thought of evangelism by means of loud speakers, distribution of tracts or mass meetings. The Khmer Evangelical Church is made up of about 1,000 Christians under the care of about a dozen pastors. These

Christians are drawn primarily from the poorer class of the population. The pastors find it necessary to pursue a secular occupation in order to live, and cannot give all the time that is desirable to their pastoral ministry. In a few places, principally in Phnom Penh, one comes across members of the Reformed Church of France; they are visited regularly by a pastor of their church.

It is easy to understand that in a situation like this, with a small number of Christians, extremely limited material resources and virtually no educated leadership, these churches cannot take in hand the universal problems with which all churches are concerned. The better elements in the Khmer Evangelical Church, however, understand that the main aim of their present activities should be a deepening of the pastoral ministry, in order to establish a solid base from which once established these churches will be able to develop and expand more readily among the population. The evangelization of Cambodia will require many, many years.

Some missionaries believe that, without abandoning the traditional methods of evangelization by means of preaching and schools, new methods have to be discovered. One such method would be the development of a Christian monasticism, based on contemplation and the life of poverty. Such monastic life would have excellent chances of appealing to the spirit and the mind of the Khmer people and would create centers from which the spirit of the gospel could radiate into the surrounding areas.

LAOS

Three million people live in Laos, where forests and mountains alternate with rice fields. Rice is the principal product, but production lags behind the needs. This is a poor country, and ceaseless troubles have gravely disturbed the efforts at economic recovery that have been made with help from abroad.

The Laotian people belong to the Thai group. But the population also includes 15,000 Chinese, 50,000 Vietnamese and a number of groups forming ethnic minorities that are either Malay or Indonesian in origin.

Traditional Beliefs

The great majority of the people are Hinayana Buddhists, as in Cambodia. Buddhism is the religion of the state, and the king is the High Protector of this religion. The national minorities have never been penetrated by Buddhism, and it is among them that the Christian gospel has had a certain amount of success.

Over the past ten years there has been a revival of Buddhism in Laos, as elsewhere in Southeast Asia. Furthermore, there is a clearly marked tendency in official circles to identify "Buddhist" and "Laotian." This presents the missionary of the gospel of Christ with a number of problems. The difficulties created by the Vietcong and the threat from communism provide many Laotians with a further reason to renew the spiritual values of Buddhism, and a certain amount of foreign propaganda directed to the same end is being carried on.

The Roman Catholic Mission

It was about the year 1630 that the first missionary managed to spend a few weeks in Vientiane; but this visit was almost without results, and was not followed up. Various other efforts followed, but each one lacked the spirit of perseverance. Only in the middle of the nineteenth century was the evangelization of Laos systematically undertaken. The starting point for the mission was Ubon in Siam (Thailand). In 1899 the Apostolic Vicariate of Laos was created, and included within its borders a part of the kingdom of Siam. There were then 8,000 Catholics, and progress has been extremely slow. The strength of Buddhism and the privileged position accorded to it create great obstacles. Furthermore, from the outset, the Christian religion seemed to be an affair of foreigners, not only because the missionaries were Europeans but also because the first converts were Vietnamese or members of the ethnic minority groups.

The war of 1940–45, the troubles that followed it, the influence of North Vietnam—all these provide a new crop of difficulties in the way of Christian work. Movement becomes ever more difficult. To hold any meeting draws attention to the church. After the Geneva Agreement of 1954, calm was restored, but calm only in a relative sense of the word; then once again, within a very short time it was anarchy all over again. The country is divided into three zones. In the northern zone the influence of North Vietnam is preponderant, and any kind of Christian work is practically impossible. A little more liberty obtains in the central zone, which is "neutral," and in the south.

Laos is divided into three Catholic dioceses, each of which has a foreign missionary bishop at its head. Catholics number 27,000, with 85 priests, of whom 77 are foreigners, and 8 Laotians or Vietnamese.

The Protestant Mission

In 1902, Mr. and Mrs. G. Contesse, of the Swiss Brethren, traveled up the Mekong River and founded the first mission station at Song Khone in lower Laos. The missionary couple immediately began to travel around, to make contact both with the Laotians and with the Khas tribesmen who lived in the vicinity. A year later another family, the Willys, arrived as reinforcements, and opened up medical and evangelistic work at Song Khone. In 1905 the missionaries experienced the joy of the first convert when Tit Pan, who had worked with them from the time of their arrival and whose help had been invaluable, received baptism. Just at this time the missionary team was strengthened further by the arrival of a third family, that of Mr. and Mrs. C. Contesse.

In 1908 Mr. G. Contesse and his wife died in a cholera epidemic. The other missionaries left the station for a few months in order to escape the danger, but then returned to Song Khone and set themselves to work again. In 1920 another epidemic broke out, and two more missionaries died. In 1926 the New Testament was published in Laotian, marking a turning point in the work of evangelization.

This handful of Swiss missionaries, whose numbers hardly ever exceeded ten, continued to work with the utmost tenacity in the face of immense difficulties. In 1952 they celebrated the jubilee of their mission and the arrival of the first missionary family. As a result of their years of labor they could count just 452 baptisms.

But from 1928 onward, they were no longer alone in the effort to bring the gospel to the people of Laos. The CMA had made contact with them and in the end it was decided that the CMA would evangelize northern Laos, and the Swiss Brethren southern Laos.

In point of fact, the area of Luang Prabang had been visited a number of times by Presbyterian missionaries from north Siam, so that when the CMA arrived they found a number of Christians, principally among the Khas, who were already being cared for by a Kha pastor. In 1929 the CMA founded a mission station at Luang Prabang, two years later a second station at Vientiane and in 1939 a station at Xieng Khouang. The success of their work has been limited, the majority of conversions having taken place among the ethnic minorities.

World War II isolated the missionaries and caused them endless difficulties. Finally, all American personnel had to leave, and their converts, amounting now to a few hundred, were left without pastoral care. After the war the missionaries returned to their stations and during the short period of relative peace following the Geneva Agreement of 1954, the CMA opened new work in Sayaboury and Ban Houei Sai. Despite the undeclared war carried on by the three rival parties in the country, and the precarious balance of neutrality and independence in Laos, the CMA has continued its work, with only occasional periods of temporary withdrawal. In 1967 they had 29 missionaries in northern Laos, 65 churches, 3,380 baptized adults, 26 national church workers (3 ordained) and a total Evangelical constituency of 10,000. In the south, 18 missionaries are still at work, in a situation which is fraught with danger. The Overseas Missionary Fellowship, when forced to leave its work in China, moved into Laos to work among the Chinese and the unevangelized tribal people. The French Reformed Church maintains a parish in Vientiane; it concerns itself with Christians who speak French, and has a few dozen members.

The tenacity of the missionaries of Christ in Laos does not make up for the paucity of their numbers. Probably the missionary methods followed so far could be entirely reconsidered with advantage. One step in this direction was taken at a consultation in Vientiane in October, 1967, where plans were laid for the Christian community in Laos to assume a greater share in building institutions necessary for the development of the life of the nation. This is to be brought about with the cooperation of the East Asia Christian Conference and the Church of Christ in Thailand, which were invited by the Evangelical Church in Laos to participate in the consultation. Initial areas of concentration for development will be education, leadership training and medical aid. These efforts in Joint Action for Mission may herald the dawn of a new day for the Christian mission in Laos.

4 SINGAPORE MALAYSIA and BRUNEI

the church in a racial melting pot

John R. Fleming

THIS CHAPTER deals with three politically distinct territories. First, there is Singapore, an island of 225 square miles and a population of approximately two million, at the southernmost tip of the Asian mainland. Singapore is now an independent, Greek-style city-state, which has a history as a British colony (since 1819), a self-governing territory within the British Commonwealth (1959) and a part of Malaysia (1963–65).

Second, there is Malaysia, created in 1963 by the union of the Federation of Malaya, since 1957 an independent country within the British Commonwealth, with the territories of Sarawak and British North Borneo (renamed Sabah), both Crown Colonies since 1946. The former Federation of Malaya, related by various treaties to Britain, is now known as West Malaysia, while Sarawak and Sabah together are known as East Malaysia.

Third, there is the small oil-rich state of Brunei (2,220 square miles and approximately 100,000 people), which refused to become part of Malaysia in 1963 and continues as a British Protected Sultanate. Historically, Brunei has been the main center of Islam in the Borneo territories, which have all been closely related to one another in racial, tribal and religious composition.

These three territories are all within the tropics; the climate is hot and humid, with abundant rainfall all the year round, and little variation in seasonal temperatures. They are lands of jungles, rivers and mountains, with rich resources of rubber, tin, palm oil and timber.

THE PEOPLES

Singapore. Singapore offers equality to all its citizens, whatever their racial backgrounds, although more than 80 percent of the population is Chinese. Ever since Sir Stamford Raffles, the founder of Singapore, began to develop it as a trading center for Southeast Asia, the Chinese have been quick to take advantage of its geographic position and facilities. In doing so, they have contributed to its development as a great city, and from Singapore it has been mainly the Chinese who have opened up the jungles of Malaya to trade and modern development. Other races in Singapore are the Malays, Indians, Pakistanis, Sikhs, Persians, Arabs, Eurasians and Europeans.

West Malaysia. The Malays, a southern Mongoloid people, are in the majority (about 49 percent of the population), the Chinese make up nearly 40 percent and Indians, Pakistanis and others around 11 percent. The Malays are

Muslims, and Islam is the official state religion of Malaysia. The Chinese are traditionally Mahayana Buddhists with admixtures of magical Taoism and Confucian ethicism and ancestor worship; but the Chinese also form the strongest body of Christians in these countries. The Indians are mostly Hindus, though a good many are Christians. But traditional beliefs are all being affected by modern education, the scientific age and the growth of a secularist point of view.

East Malaysia. In Sarawak, the Sea Dyaks or Ibans are in the majority (about 32 percent), the Chinese are next with more than 30 percent and are increasing rapidly. Malays are just over 17 percent, and the rest are Land Dyaks and other tribal groups. The Dyaks and other indigenous peoples are originally animists and head hunters, but there is now a strong Christian movement among them.

Sabah. The Kadazans are the largest group and like other indigenous people are animists, living in the rural areas with a low standard of living. The Chinese live mainly in the towns and are merchants and shopkeepers. The Malays are Muslims, occupied mainly in fishing, boat building and rice growing. The rest of the population is made up of Filipinos, Indians, Indonesians, Europeans and other small groups.

Brunei. The Malays are over 65 percent, the Chinese around 20 percent and Indians, Europeans and others make up the balance.

ROMAN CATHOLIC CHRISTIANITY

Christianity came to Malaya first with the Portuguese forces who captured Malacca in 1511. In 1641 the Protestant Dutch captured Malacca from the Portuguese and for the next 150 years Roman Catholics were persecuted until the British took over Malacca from the Dutch in 1824 and religious freedom was granted. Meanwhile Penang, which Captain Francis Light had annexed for the British in 1786, had become the main Roman Catholic missionary center.

Similarly, after Raffles had obtained Singapore for the British in a deal with the Dutch in 1819, the possibilities in this new center attracted settlers from Malacca and elsewhere in Malaya, as well as Chinese merchants from South China.

Since these early beginnings, the Roman Catholic Church has developed in West Malaysia and Singapore. The area became an archbishopric in 1953, with a French archbishop and two Malaysian bishops, and a Christian community of about 120,000. Today many new parishes and a widespread educational system are being developed.

In Sarawak, Sabah and Brunei the Roman Catholic Church was founded and developed through the Mill Hill Fathers, from 1881 when four fathers accompanied by a French priest and a Chinese catechist from Singapore arrived in Kuching, facing the dangers of the jungle and the head hunters. There are now three vicariates—Sabah including Brunei, Kuching and Miri—with more than 100,000 members and many schools and welfare institutions.

PROTESTANT CHRISTIANITY

The term "Protestant" is not altogether satisfactory to describe all non-Roman Christianity, since it will here include Mar Thoma and Syrian Orthodox Christians and some Anglicans, especially in the Diocese of Kuching (Sarawak), who do not particularly like to be called Protestant.

At any rate, there are a great number and variety of non-

Roman churches, and it would be impossible to deal with their origins and history in any detail. They are Methodist, Anglican, Chinese Christian Church, English Presbyterian, Mar Thoma, Syrian Orthodox, Baptist, Lutheran, Evangelical Lutheran, the Basel Church, the Salvation Army, the Seventh Day Adventists, and several missionary fellowships such as the Overseas Missionary Fellowship and the Borneo Evangelical Mission. Because the origins of many of these churches have affected their development and ethos even up to the present, it will be necessary to take a closer look at the beginnings of Christianity in the major denominational families, though without going into great detail.

Anglican

Like Roman Catholicism, Protestantism began in Malaysia and Singapore in relation to colonial developments. When Penang and Singapore were opened up, the East India Company appointed Church of England chaplains in Penang (1805) and in Singapore (1826).

The first St. Andrew's Church in Singapore (since 1870, St. Andrew's Cathedral) was originally planned for the use of the whole Protestant community in Singapore (1837), but through some breakdown in ecumenical relationships at that time the building was actually consecrated by the Anglican bishop of Calcutta.

The East India Company forbade its chaplains to engage in any sort of missionary work among "the natives," but many of the chaplains themselves appealed to the Society for the Propagation of the Gospel (SPG) to send men for this work. The colonial congregations also started work among the Chinese and Indians, and a local Anglican mission to the Asian population was set up in 1856. In the late nineteenth century more chaplaincy and mission work was developed in the Malay peninsula, but it progressed very slowly, hampered by financial and manpower difficulties.

The three and a half years of Japanese occupation from February, 1942 brought Asian leadership to the front and convinced the church that it must become more indigenous and train its own clergy. This new orientation has been changing the character of the church from a church of immigrants (English, Chinese or Indian) to a multiracial church for the nation. Movements toward self-government have developed, and in 1966 the first Asian bishop of West Malaysia and Singapore was consecrated. The Anglican constituency in these territories is approaching 30,000, with 45 local clergy and 15 missionary clergy. The church has developed a good number of schools and some medical work. Its influence on individuals in the political and commercial world has been considerable.

By contrast, in Sarawak and Sabah, the "Anglican Church of Borneo" planned mission work from the beginning of its establishment in Kuching, Sarawak in 1848. Chaplaincy work was developed in various centers, such as Kuching and Sandakan in North Borneo (1882), and missionary work among the indigenous peoples and the Chinese was also vigorously carried out. Francis Thomas McDougall, Bishop of Labuan and Sarawak, played a notable part in these advances. There is now an Anglican constituency in Sarawak of over 20,000, with 20 trained clergy, of whom half are indigenous, mainly Chinese.

Since 1962 Sabah has been a separate diocese, with an Anglican constituency of around 6,000 mainly among the Chinese, a Chinese bishop and twelve clergy. A mission to the Kadazans (or Dusuns) was started ten years ago.

Presbyterian, Congregational and Chinese Christian Church

The London Missionary Society (now the Congregational Council for World Mission) sent the first missionary, William Milne, to Malaya in 1814. When in 1843 China was opening up to foreigners, the LMS closed down their "Ultra-Ganges station" in Malaya and ordered their personnel to Hong Kong. One missionary, Benjamin Keasberry, however, refused to leave his work in Singapore, resigned and became a self-supporting missionary, and until his death in 1875 carried out a faithful and active ministry among the Malays and the Malay-speaking Chinese in Singapore. This was one of the few efforts in Malaysia to establish Christian work among the Malay people.

At just about this time, when the LMS mission was closed down, the Presbyterian settlers and businessmen in Singapore petitioned the Presbyterian Mission in Calcutta and the Church in Scotland to send Presbyterian ministers for work among the European settlers. From this has developed the work of the Presbyterian Church of England and of its Malaysia Presbytery, with work in Singapore, Kuala Lumpur, Ipoh and Penang, mainly among European planters, tin miners, businessmen, managers and clerks.

The Singapore congregation, founded in 1856, collaborated with Keasberry in work among the Chinese, and as a result the first congregation of the Chinese Christian Church began at Bukit Timah on the island of Singapore. Work among the Chinese, however, did not really develop until the arrival of J. A. B. Cook in 1881. In 40 years work in Singapore, and with never more than one or two missionary colleagues, he laid a good foundation for the development that took place in the first 40 years of the twentieth century. During that time, there was extensive immigration of many Chinese to Singapore and Malaya, because of a big demand for Chinese labor. Among the workers and merchants were many Christians, and the Chinese church in south China sent preachers and pastors who became the leaders of the Chinese church in Singapore and Malaya. In the years immediately after World War II, this church was part of the Church of Christ in China. Then, when the Communists took over China, it became the Singapore-Malaysia Synod of the Chinese Christian Church, with cordial missionary relationships with the English Presbyterian Mission, the London Missionary Society (now the CCWM) and the Reformed Church of America Mission. This church today is fully autonomous; it has 48 congregations in Singapore and Malaysia and a Christian community of about 18,000, with 25 Chinese and 8 missionary clergy.

Methodist

The latest of the larger denominations has been the fastest growing. Methodism came to Singapore and Malaysia in 1885 with the Englishman William F. Oldham, who was supported by the American Methodist Church. Through a policy of developing a large educational program throughout the country, this church has had a particularly large influence on the new generations. Today Methodism in Singapore and West Malaysia numbers 25,000 in 125 congregations, with 122 government grant-aided schools, 95 clergy and a supporting missionary staff of 26, including the present bishop.

In the period 1900–40, the question of staffing and running schools was important to the church, to the neglect of building up strong congregations in themselves. The Japanese occupation and the demands of postwar rehabilitation, as well as the growing concern in the country for strengthening the new nation, changed all this. The need for local leadership in the church became clear, as in other churches, and The Methodist Church has been a strong partner in the efforts to train an indigenous ministry at Trinity Theological College in Singapore, since that institution was founded in 1948.

Methodist work has developed along four lines: 1) Among the so-called "Straits Chinese," descendants of the original Chinese settlers in Singapore, Malacca and Penang (the Straits Settlements), both Malay and English speaking. This work began in 1894, and now only the Methodists and the Brethren have Malay speaking congregations, though Malay is the official national language of Malaysia. 2) Tamil speaking churches, which are now also largely English speaking. Tens of thousands of Indians came to Singapore and Malaysia in the early 1900's from Tamil speaking South India and North Ceylon, to work as laborers on the railways and rubber plantations. Many were already Christian. By 1914 they had their own Methodist Church administration; and now they are part of the English language Malayan Annual Conference. Their people are English educated and English speaking, but their Tamil language is still maintained as a strong cultural link. 3) Chinese speaking churches. Like other churches in Singapore and Malaysia, the Methodists have developed strong Chinese congregations among the Chinese immigrants to the country. Previously, these immigrants had hoped to return to China. Now more and more they are citizens of the country, and their character as transient immigrants has changed. One problem here is that the Chinese speak many dialects, and church organization has followed the vernacular languages, though Chinese national language (Mandarin) has been taught in Chinese schools in Malaya and Singapore since 1926. 4) The Wesley churches, which are English speaking congregations and originally ministered to Europeans, as did the Anglican and Presbyterian chaplaincies. Over the years, however, the membership of these churches has increasingly been made up of English speaking Asians, both Chinese and Indians, as well as many Eurasians. Until a few years ago, these congregations were led by United States missionaries but now almost all have indigenous locally trained ministers.

In Sarawak, Methodist work began in 1900 when a boat load of about 1,000 Chinese, mostly Methodists, arrived from Fukien Province in South China under the leadership of one Wong Nai Siong. These "Chinese Pilgrim Fathers" left the difficult situation in China created by the Boxer Rebellion and its anti-Christian movement, to seek a new beginning in the land that the White Rajah James Brooke, ruler of Sarawak, was making available. From this nucleus, and after great hardships, developed a vigorous work among the Chinese, and later among the indigenous peoples, the former head-hunting Sea Dyaks or Ibans in their longhouses. With its center at Sibu, the church has grown and spread up and down the great Rejang River and its tributaries. There is now a Methodist Chinese Conference with a constituency of about 17,000, and also an Iban Provisional Conference with 13,000, which are among the fastest-growing churches in the region. There are 39 Chinese clergy and 12 Ibans, with a seminary at Sibu for educating both groups of ministers.

Churches of the Indian "Dispersion"

Mention has already been made of the development of Indian churches among the Anglicans and Methodists. Other churches that have been at work among the Indians are the Mar Thoma Syrian Church, the Orthodox Syrian Church and the Tamil Evangelical Lutheran Church (since 1962 the Evangelical Lutheran Church in Malaysia). These churches have grown as their parent churches in India have accepted pastoral responsibility for Indian Christians moving to Malaysia and Singapore as estate laborers, road workers, shopkeepers and traders. Together they number about 4,000 communicants and a total Christian community of more than 12,000.

Other Groups

The Seventh Day Adventists, with their East Asia headquarters in Singapore, have a number of congregations and schools in Singapore, West Malaysia, East Malaysia and Brunei; also hospitals in Singapore and Penang and a Bible seminary in Singapore. Their constituency is around 3,000, in 20 congregations.

The Bible Presbyterian Church is a small Chinese church of a few congregations, with work also in English, a breakaway in the mid-1950's from the Chinese Christian Church and linked with the antiecumenical "McIntire faction" and the International Council of Churches of Christ. Its vigorous missionary vocation and its strong sense of stewardship challenge the other churches.

The Baptist Church is located mainly in Singapore and West Malaysia, though there are some recently founded churches in Sabah in East Malaysia. Since 1951 the Southern Baptists from the United States have been associated with these local Baptist churches, providing no less than 53 missionaries for Chinese and English work and enabling them to develop a small seminary in Penang, a bookstore and a retreat and recreation center.

The Salvation Army, its headquarters in Singapore, started work there in 1935 and has centers now in West Malaysia and in Kuching, Sarawak. During the Japanese occupation all work was suspended, but it was reopened in 1945. They now have a Christian community of around 1,500, with 38 full-time officers.

The Basel Christian Church of Malaysia (formerly the Basel Christian Mission) began with the immigration of Hakka-speaking Chinese from Canton Province in South China to North Borneo around 1882. This church has spread mainly along the west coast rural areas of Sabah and the main urban centers of Jesselton and Sandakan, and now numbers between 7,000 and 8,000 in 20 congregations. Mainly a Chinese church, it has been autonomous since 1925, but at present has only five ordained ministers. Since 1952, work has been carried on also among the indigenous Dusuns, resulting in 17 congregations, with 1,500 Christians and 1,800 catechumens.

Brief mention must also be made of two important missionary groups. The first is the Overseas Missionary Fellowship, which came into Singapore and Malaya in 1952 when their work in China was closed down. Their world headquarters has now been established in Singapore, and some 163 missionaries are working in Singapore and Malaysia. Recently their strategy has changed to concentrate work on the main centers of population, whereas in the 1950's when they arrived in the country they were mainly working in the

ecial "new villages" set up by the government at that
me as a defence against the Communist guerrilla threat
Malaya. In towns where there are already churches, the
olicy of this group has been to work with individual con-
regations or clergy whose "evangelical faith" was akin to
eir own, and to loan personnel to other denominations
nd agencies for cooperation at the local level.

The other mission group is the Borneo Evangelical Mis-
on, founded in 1928 for work in the Borneo jungles among
ne tribes. Now, with more than 50 missionaries from Aus-
alia, New Zealand, and the United Kingdom, the plan is
establish self-supporting and self-propagating churches
each tribal group within 15 years of the time of begin-
ing work. The Evangelical Church of Borneo (that is, in
arawak and Sabah) has now been formed from this work,
rawing its membership from 10 tribes, with a total Chris-
an constituency of 30,000 in some 200 congregations. They
ave more than 100 pastors supported by the churches they
erve. These tribal men and women church workers are
ained in a four-year course in a Bible school. Missionaries
re engaged in Bible translation in seven languages, Bible
eaching programs and evangelism, and literature produc-
on and distribution. They make considerable use of air-
raft for mobility in this jungle land. Back of this work is the
xperience of the ten years 1928–38, when a movement
pread from the Murut Christians in Indonesian Borneo
Kalimantan), converts of the Christian and Missionary
lliance, across the borders to the Muruts in Sarawak, a
otoriously drunken and debased group which the Sarawak
overnment fully believed would soon die out. When mis-
ionaries returned in 1946 after the Japanese occupation,
hey found a new Murut tribe—self-respecting, hard work-

ing and concerned for the spread of the gospel. This is on
of the most fascinating and powerful stories of moder
church history anywhere.

We should also mention the Bible Societies of Malaysia
with their headquarters in Singapore, which support, wit
the help of the British and Foreign Bible Society and th
National Bible Society of Scotland, the translation and dis
tribution of the Scriptures in the many languages of thes
territories. The Bible Societies have their first local genera
secretary and are moving toward greater indigenous suppor
and autonomy.

From this brief account of the development of th
churches, we now turn to the major factors in the presen
situation.

THE SITUATION TODAY

The situation in which the churches exist today is vastl
different even from the early 1950's when the present write
came to Singapore and Malaya.

On the *political* side, the nationalism that is common t
all Asian countries and is probably the main driving forc
of the so-called Asian Revolution has led to the establish
ment first of independent Malaya in 1957 and self-govern
ing Singapore in 1959, and then of the wider union of Ma
laysia, including Singapore, Sarawak and British Nort
Borneo, in 1963. This development led to Indonesian oppo
sition and the establishment of "confrontation" betwee
Indonesia and the new nation, involving them in mutually
harmful cessation of trade, communications and diplomati
relations, and actual warfare in the jungles of Borneo. For
tunately, this *"Konfrontasi"* has now ended with the chang
of government in Djakarta, and relationships between In

onesia and Malaysia and Singapore are being built up again. In 1965, however, Singapore's government, with a strong and effective Socialist interracial and interreligious policy, was forced out of Malaysia by the conservative and Muslim forces in the Kuala Lumpur government. Sarawak and Sabah, with Muslim minorities and large groups of Chinese and indigenous peoples, are both suspicious of Kuala Lumpur's Malay-privileges policy, in a multiracial nation, though certain safeguards were written into the Constitution on these points as they affect the Borneo territories.

Singapore continues as an independent island republic, with one of the most efficient and graft-free governments in the whole of Asia.

Brunei, never part of Malaysia, is notable as the home ground of the rebel Azahari who fought against Malaysia on the Indonesian side during the "Confrontation" because he favored a federation of the Borneo states rather than a link-up with Malaya.

The biggest task now is nation building. The difficult economic problem of providing full rice bowls for the people is aggravated by the population explosion and the fact that more than half the population is under 25. Family planning programs now have government backing in Malaysia and Singapore, and this will have some effect. But sheer numbers are bound to increase, making more imperative than ever vigorous planning of economic development and industrialization. Malaysia, with its natural resources of rubber, tin and timber, has sufficient economic stability to attract capital from abroad. Sabah and Sarawak are still largely rural and underdeveloped, and from the point of view of the people in these two states, the success or fail-

ure of Malaysia will depend on the central government
ability to solve the economic problems. Singapore, whic
has long experience in providing the services needed in
great trading center and port, is developing new industrie
at the new industrial satellite town of Jurong, which it i
hoped will provide for about 400,000 people when it i
fully developed. This should take care of some of the in
creasing numbers of educated youngsters coming out c
schools and colleges every year.

Education is vital, and vast sums are being spent in a
the territories on education of various kinds. There is a
irresistible demand for education on the part of the people
New schools are continually going up, universities are ex
panding, and teacher training facilities are being develope
on ever-larger scales. Colleges are being planned for Sara
wak and Sabah. At present, there are more Singapore an
Malaysian students in universities overseas than in th
three universities within these territories.

Particularly in Singapore, there is a race against time, t
provide job opportunities for the increasing numbers o
trained citizens. The hidden element in the situation, th
underground Communist party, is ready to foment labo
unrest and create trouble for the Prime Minister, Mr. Le
Kuan Yew, the one Asian politician who has met the Com
munists head-on and bested them.

Unfortunately, political and economic tension exists be
tween the governments of Malaysia and Singapore. In a situa
tion demanding cooperation, integration of economies an
a common market, there are now trade barriers, protectiv
taxes and separate currencies!

In the area of *races* and *religions*, there are serious prob
lems and potential trouble. In Malaysia, the Malays ar

politically dominant, and under the Constitution they have certain economic and political privileges in the new state. At the same time, the slightly smaller number of Chinese in the nation are economically dominant, both in East and West Malaysia. The Malays are Muslim, and Islam is the official religion in Malaysia. In the period of British influence in Malaya, the policy was "hands off" the Malays and their religion. Christian work could develop among the Chinese, Indians and other migrant peoples. The more indigenous peoples, however, the Malays, were protected from the teachings of any other faith by the Sultans' powers to ban any Christian caught trying to convert a Malay. A Malay Christian convert, of whom there have been very few in Malaya though more in Singapore and Borneo, was likely to lose his job, be ejected from his family and have his life threatened. This traditional situation was confirmed in the 1957 Malaya and the 1963 Malaysia Constitutions. In the case of the Borneo territories of Sarawak and Sabah, where there were many indigenous peoples (Sea Dyaks or Ibans, Muruts and others) who were Christians, as well as strong Chinese Christian churches, some safeguards were written into the Constitution. These were intended to maintain the existing freedom of religion and to prevent any change in the constitutional *status quo* without a two-thirds majority in the legislative councils of the states.

Singapore, 80 percent Chinese, with a religion that is traditionally an amalgam of animism, Mahayana Buddhism, Confucian ancestor reverence and moralism, and the more superstitious forms of Taoism, is now developing constitutionally as a secular state with a multiracial multireligious policy, and providing for equal rights for all citizens. This is one of the most interesting and potentially influential experiments in racial harmony and cooperation anywhere in the world. If two million people in an island of 225 square miles—Chinese, Indians, Pakistanis, Sikhs, Malays, Singhalese, Persians, Arabs, Eurasians, Europeans and others, with their different Buddhist, Hindu, Muslim, Sikh, Christian and other religions—can create a harmonious multicultural city-state guaranteeing the essential freedoms to all citizens, with a viable economy, it could have wide repercussions not only in Asia but elsewhere. This need not result in mere religious communalism. It could also mean real efforts on the part of citizens of different religions to understand each other, and each other's faiths, at a deep level. Certainly Christianity has nothing to fear from this.

CONTEMPORARY CHALLENGES TO THE CHURCHES

1. There is first of all the challenge to a wider and deeper understanding of mission and evangelism.

Nurtured for the most part on traditions of individual pietism and nonsocially or politically involved Christianity, Christians today are being challenged to see nation building as the area in which God is at work in his Holy Spirit, where they must be obedient to him and try to be a sign of his presence and purpose. Christians are no longer transient immigrants in the nation. They belong here, and they must relate the gospel to where they are. This means the presence and obedience of Christian laymen and women in the many-sided activities of the nation's life. It means Christian politicians and civil servants of honesty, integrity and vocation; labor union leaders and workers with a sense of responsibility to the community as a whole; managers appreciative of the rights of workers; citizens with a strong sense of what constitutes the common good.

This challenge is slowly being understood and accepted. Some churches have started lay training courses, so that laymen and women can understand the faith better and know where it must be acted out in the present situation. In Sarawak, strong Christian influences were exerted in the interests of constitutional freedoms at the time of the state's entry into Malaysia. In Singapore, the churches have together taken significant action to support constitutional changes so that all citizens have equality before the law and the same rights and privileges. In politics, in the various territories, there are Christian politicians and civil servants who in the church, and as the church, are learning again or for the first time what Christian vocation is. And the same is true of other spheres of life.

But this understanding of the fullness or totality of mission that is laid on Christ's people has to battle against much opposition—not so much from people outside the church, as from those who are in it, who prefer a more "spiritual" and detached kind of Christianity!

2. With the independence of Singapore and Malaysia and the emergence of national leaders in both countries, the churches have been forced to look seriously at their own autonomy and indigenous leadership. Here they have discovered dependency in church government, finances and personnel. In colonial times, it was natural to look elsewhere for help—to London, or New York, or Canterbury. Now, as churches in independent sovereign states, they have to understand what the autonomy of a church in and for the nation means. The answers, now slowly emerging, are that the four conferences of The Methodist Church in Malaysia and Singapore have voted to become autonomous, that is, not under the jurisdiction of the Methodist General

Conference in the United States, by 1968. Anglicans are seeking to form a province of at least three dioceses so that they can cease to be "missionary dioceses," and become fully independent within the Anglican family. The two Lutheran churches in Malaysia have recently ceased to be "missions" and have become Malaysian churches. Similarly, since the 1950's the local churches in Malaya and Singapore have been training their own ministers at Trinity Theological College, and five churches are cooperating now in this venture—Methodists, Anglicans, Chinese Christian Church and the two Lutheran churches. The graduates[1] of this united training program are increasingly assuming responsible positions in their respective churches, and can speak also as citizens of the new nations. The government of Malaysia has recently assisted this movement toward indigenous leadership by putting a limit of 10 years on the time a foreign missionary may serve in Malaysia! The Anglican Church in West Malaysia and Singapore has just elected the first local bishop, the Rt. Rev. Chiu Ban It, and the Council of Churches of Malaysia and Singapore has since January 1967 had its first local-born general secretary.

3. Obviously, this whole situation holds a challenge for Christian unity and church union. While one must give thanks for the missionary zeal that brought Christianity to these territories, the account just given is frightening in its picture of divided churches seeking to perpetuate their divisions in Asia! What is the Asian convert to think? Unfortunately, the converts for the most part have accepted the divisions quite cheerfully, and have settled down in

---

[1] Now numbering 152 of whom 107 are still in full-time church work. Of the 44 women graduates, many have married, but still have opportunities to serve. A considerable number are ministers' wives!

them! But there are other signs too. As elsewhere, the pressures of fresh biblical thinking about the *church* as the one people of God, its common heritage and its one mission in and to the world, has been influential, particularly since the 1950's, when faith and order discussions among the churches in Malaysia and Singapore began. To intensify the urgency of this question, the political situation in the territories has also been exerting pressures. Government will listen to a "church" voice, but not to a host of divided churches. Government policy is to create unity in the nation, in both Singapore and Malaysia, out of many races. Churches are obliged to question themselves and ask if they are really a sign of God's new humanity in Christ, when they are so separated from one another, and even in one denomination are divided into different language congregations.

At any rate, the pressure is on, and the main churches in West Malaysia and Singapore were challenged at the end of 1965 to state, within a year, whether they seriously intended to enter into negotiations for church union. It appears that five churches will go ahead with this plan, and they together make up the majority of Christians in the territory. In Sarawak, the Anglican diocese is "high church" and is unlikely to welcome church union, but in Sabah, there is a good prospect that the Anglicans will join in. The Methodists in Sarawak, as part of an autonomous church of Malaysia and Singapore, will probably come in too, if the plan proceeds.

4. In the area of church cooperation, as distinct from plans for church union, there has been a significant development in the Council of Churches, founded in 1948 (as the Malayan Christian Council). Slowly the principle of joint

action, "to do all things together except what conscience compels us to do separately," has come to exert more and more influence on the churches. Joint planning for ministry in new housing and industrial areas; joint university chaplaincies; joint counseling services; joint approaches to government—these have all been happening. The big issue is to get the member churches of the Council of Churches to use that organization not simply for "marginal operations" but for the normal, ordinary and essential work of the churches together, such as lay training, church membership training, evangelism, Christian education, literature production and so on. The concept of the Council of Churches in the minds of its member churches is too often that of an extra, dispensable organization, in comparison to the "real work" of the denominations. The East Asia Christian Conference, with its recent emphasis on Joint Action for Mission, has been exerting some pressure on local thinking in this regard.

In relation to Roman Catholics, since Vatican II there have been some meetings between Roman Catholics and Protestants, such as the joint public service of worship and witness in the Week of Prayer for Christian Unity, and some cordial personal relationships. But real conversations about the common task facing all the churches have scarcely begun. The documents coming out of the 1966 East Asia Christian Conference Faith and Order meeting at Hong Kong give some useful information and guidance for local churches. Conversations are also needed with the "conservative evangelicals" who, existing in most churches and strongly influencing certain denominations, tend not to favor joint ecumenical operations or church union. The theological suspicions lying behind this must be dissipated by the kind of conversations which took place, for the whole East Asia area, at the Bangkok General Assembly of the EACC in January 1968.

5. New approaches to mission and service. Traditionally, the churches in Malaysia and Singapore have pioneered in a great many ways: in the school system, girls' education, welfare among the aborigines of the Malayan highlands; agricultural training for the Ibans in Sarawak; hospitals, clinics, schools for the blind etc. Now these forms of service are recognized as the responsibility and duty of the state, and though the churches may play a part in these spheres, they are no longer the main agents. This is good. It means that governments recognize that they must provide these services for all citizens. It means also that the churches, instead of trying to compete and to run expensive institutions of their own, must concentrate on turning out men and women of true Christian vocation to serve in government institutions, where they can be a sign of what it means to be the church in the world. The churches must also be sensitive to areas of human need of which governments are not yet aware, or about which they are unable or unwilling to take action.

New forms of witness and service need to be developed. Examples are a new counseling service offered jointly by an Anglican and Methodist team in Singapore; the telephone "life line service" for people in despair; and church involvement in the state family planning association. In addition, from 1950–57, during the "Emergency Period," the churches in Malaya sent their people, both missionaries and nationals, to live in the "new villages" along with the Chinese settlers gathered into them from the jungle edges as a security measure against the Communist guerrillas.

As to new patterns of mission, attention has already been drawn to the policy of the Borneo Evangelical Mission in Sabah and Sarawak (though their strategy is not entirely new), where they are giving themselves 15 years to help a tribe to understand the gospel and organize its Christian life in its own fashion, without dependence on the missionary society. This is very significant, in view of the obvious weaknesses that have occurred in the Malaysian-Singapore churches as a result of prolonged dependence on Western mission bodies, for finance, personnel and policy decisions.

At Petaling Jaya, the new satellite town of Malaysia's capital Kuala Lumpur, a center has been established on an ecumenical basis (but with particular Lutheran support) to promote mission in the new society by more adequate training of Christian laity. This is one of the most promising experiments in mission at the present time. Another form of mission is just beginning at Jurong, Singapore, where a team ministry is planned, with members from different denominations, to develop new approaches to industrial plants and to unions and management. It is too early to say how these will develop. Another new form of mission has been the "frontier internship" in the Nanyang (Chinese) University on Singapore Island, and new noninstitutional approaches of "Christian presence" to student organizations.

In the rural areas of West Malaysia, under the aegis of the Council of Churches, a mobile training team with members drawn from different denominations is engaged in experiments in training lay leadership for rural churches that have no resident pastor. This has been named "Operation *oikodome*," from the New Testament Greek word that means the *up-building* of the churches.

One "new" form of mission that is urgently needed in

Malaysia and Singapore is a more serious effort to understand Islam and the other Asian religions. Christians need to understand their neighbors of other faiths, and of no faith. Something of this is done, of course, in the training of clergy at Trinity Theological College. But more needs to be done in the normal work of congregations, not for dogmatic battle as the politicians fear, but to understand where the different faiths lead men in the contemporary revolution and fast-changing world. Here, if the church understands its own mission to society, there can be a more effective and related presentation of the Christian gospel in contemporary society. There are some hopes of the churches setting up an ecumenical center in Singapore where this kind of activity and other similar "studies for action" can take place.

PROSPECTS

It is difficult to predict the future of Christianity in Singapore and Malaysia. Powerful forces are working against its advance: the widely spreading secularism that has rejected the old faiths of Asia and all religion; Islam, the official religion of Malaysia with considerable government financial resources behind it; and a widely prevalent local cultural attitude, which may be referred to as *"tidapah-ism,"* [2] signifying a spirit of drift or putting off decisions because nothing matters.

Even more important are the forces within the church itself, working against its true mission and function of salt, leaven, or light in society. These include narrow, self-preserving interests that keep the church back from intense involvement in the life of "the world"; a mistaken pietism

[2] Malay *tidapah*—it doesn't matter.

that thinks of the Christian faith as a puritan religion which has to do only with the individual's own private life, and not with God's purpose for all men in their relationships and society; a static understanding of the church and its life and work, afraid of new patterns and structures of Christian living and of congregational life; forms of worship that are dead but not buried, which cannot provide dynamic spiritual nurture for Christian obedience and real fellowship in the Christian task; failure to give adequate teaching and training to the many who come into the faith only to fall away later; and a general failure to be open to the movement of God's Spirit in the rapidly changing situation where he is shaking the foundations.

Yet in a changing world lies also the great ground of hope. God is active, working out his age-long purpose for men and nations. Where the church, firmly based on the gospel of God's re-creating love in Jesus Christ, is open to his leading and obedient to his purpose, there is hope. There are signs of the Holy Spirit's working in Malaysia and Singapore, in national policies making for a fuller and freer life for all men; and there are also signs of his presence renewing his people in their understanding of the gospel, their Christian calling, their mission, their unity and their obedience.

As a minority faith, faced by great challenges in society and by serious weaknesses in its own life—what chance does Christianity have? Humanly, little. Yet its life lies not in "chance," but in God's purpose. It is his will that all men come to the faith and find life. This is the church's expectant hope in mission, whether in Singapore and Malaysia or in the United States and Europe.

5 INDONESIA

social revolution and christian renewal

Frank L. Cooley

AMERICANS ARE often surprised to learn that Indonesia is one of the largest nations of the world. In total land area (738,865 square miles) it ranks fourteenth. In population (112 million) it ranks fifth. They are more surprised to discover that the Christian church in Indonesia is one of the largest in Asia and perhaps the fastest growing in the world.

THE SETTING

Indonesia is a far-flung archipelago. Indonesians call it their *Tanah-Air*, their "land-water." Most of it is water, though land area comprises more than 3,000 islands. The country's unusual geographic diversity—deep straits and wide seas separating islands, high volcanic mountain ranges,

heavy tropical rain forests and wide swampy seacoasts—
has kept groups of people relatively isolated. The result is a
great diversity of societies and cultures. Indonesia's present
condition and her main problem are symbolized in the national motto: *Bhinneka Tunggal Ika*, "Diversity Becoming
Unity."

There are also, however, important forces that bind together the various Indonesian peoples. Almost all belong to
one racial stock and family of languages. They have experienced similar external influences, especially colonial rule.
Most important of all, since 1945 they have struggled together in the revolution to attain and protect their independence from the Dutch.

From India came the first external influences. Early in
the Christian era Indian cultural elements entered western
Indonesia, and by the eighth century Hinduism and Buddhism had become deeply rooted. An amalgam of these new
religions with the cultures of Sumatra and Java provided
the basis for extensive and powerful empires from the
seventh to the fifteenth centuries. The societies that flowered
then produced magnificent cultural monuments in stone, in
musical, dramatic, dance and literary forms and in moral,
mystical and ceremonial systems.

Traders from western Asia brought the first influences of
Islam in the twelfth century. By the sixteenth century, on
the eve of Western penetration, Islam had become widely
accepted in Sumatra, Java and the coastal areas of the other
large islands. It profoundly influenced the way of life
in the Atjeh and Minangkabau regions of Sumatra, in western Java and Madura, in southern Sulawesi (Celebes),
Lombok, Sumbawa and the northern Moluccas. In central
and eastern Java, by contrast, Islam entered less deeply,

king the form of a veneer on the Hindu-Javanese culture.
oday, the Indonesian people are about 85 percent Islamic
religion, but they distinguish between *Islam fanatik*
zealous Muslims) and *Islam statistik* (nominal Muslims).
Islam forced Hinduism, as a distinct religion, out of Java
Bali, where it fused with the indigenous Balinese religion.
oday the Bali-Hindu religion with two million adherents
one of the government-recognized religions of Indonesia,
long with Islam and Christianity.

During the sixteenth century Christianity appeared as
art of Western expansion into Asia. First the Portuguese,
ccompanied by Roman Catholic priests, and later the
Dutch, accompanied by Reformed ministers, established
ade footholds. These expanded into military and political
dministrations that gradually brought the archipelago
nder colonial subjugation, a process completed by 1910.
Western cultural influences brought changes that disrupted
ng-accepted ways of life. As access to political and eco-
omic participation and power became increasingly the
onopoly of foreigners, a sense of injustice and inferiority
d Indonesians to revolution. Political revolution won in-
ependence from colonial subjection, declared on August
7, 1945, but still fought for until December, 1949. Since
950 Indonesia has sought, by trial and error, a political
ystem by which the people can build a new nation. A
eriod of parliamentary democracy was superseded in 1959
y President Sukarno's "guided democracy." In 1966 this
nded in violence when it appeared to the people to be
ading to communism. Now major emphasis is being given
the long-neglected economy of the nation.

Beneath dramatic political events and longed-for eco-
omic development flow strong currents of social and cul-

tural revolution. Revolution means transformation. Tran
formation means modernization. Social groupings and inst
tutions are undergoing radical change, as are the norm
values, expectations and attitudes that underlie the life vie
and world view of the Indonesian people. In the process
abandoning the old and building something new and bette
which of the conflicting ideas, values and principles sha
be embraced?

What can the Christian churches contribute to the pro
ess of nation building?

THE CHURCHES

The "household of God" in Indonesia is one in the inter
of the Lord, but to the world its divisions are more evider
than its oneness. To distinguish between Roman Catholi
and Protestant churches, Indonesians speak of "the Catholi
Church" and "the Christian Church," the latter meanin
Protestant. Protestants number three times the Roma
Catholics.

Three-fourths of the Protestants are members of the 3
regional churches that make up the Indonesia Council c
Churches (DGI). This part of the Protestant community
exceeding four million, is distributed among more tha
7,000 congregations in all 25 provinces of Indonesia.

A third category of Christians, besides the Roman Cathc
lics and the Protestants in churches belonging to the DGI
includes Protestant bodies that are not members of th
DGI. They are as numerous as the conciliar churches, com
prising one grouping only for purposes of analysis. In prac
tice they fall into five groups, with a total constituency o
perhaps one million.

The first includes the Salvation Army, which entered In

onesia in 1894, and the Overseas Missionary Fellowship,
hich came in the early 1950's. These cooperate with the
GI but do not consider themselves churches.

The second is a group of churches and bodies similar to
lose within the Council. Most of them developed from
preign missionary activity after World War I. The more
mportant ones are: The Christian and Missionary Alliance
CMA), an American-based effort entering Indonesia in
929; the "Go Ye Fellowship"; the "World Evangelization
lrusade"; and a Netherlands-based Christian Reformed
roup, all working mostly in east Indonesia.

The third is a group of schismatic bodies originating from
ndonesian churches. They generally have no relations with
nissionary societies outside Indonesia. In most cases, the
auses of schism were nontheological. Several have applied
or membership in the DGI.

The fourth group is often referred to by Indonesian
hurchmen as *bidaat*, literally sects, viewed as living around
he edge of Indonesian churches, from which they often
ttract members. Among them are the Southern Baptist
lhurch from the United States, which came in 1952 and
oncentrates on Java, and numerous Pentecostal groups,
ome based in Europe and some in America, which spread
uite rapidly in Java, northern Celebes and eastern Indo-
lesia following World War I. Considerable splitting from
vithin has characterized the Pentecostals in Indonesia. The
lmerican-based Assemblies of God and Seventh Day Adventists fall in this fourth grouping, which emphasizes
vangelistic methods common in the United States and,
specially among the Pentecostals, the spiritual healing of
llness. Three of the older Pentecostal churches have be-
ome members of the DGI in recent years.

A fifth type, which has a debatable relationship to Chris
tianity, includes groups in Batakland (*Bijbelkring*) an
Nias (*Faawosa*) that manifest syncretism between Chris
tian and indigenous religion, as well as the Jehovah's Wit
nesses and Christian Science. These groups are small an
do not seem to be growing.

Roman Catholicism is the oldest form of Christianity i
Indonesia. Catholic missions began in the Moluccas (th
Spice Islands, eastern Indonesia) in the 1530's under Portu
guese protection. Francis Xavier spent most of 1546 ther
helping lay a foundation for a promising beginning by th
Franciscans, Jesuits, Dominicans and other orders. Shar
opposition from Islamic forces in Atjeh and the Molucca
produced Indonesia's first Christian martyrs. Even so, b
the end of the sixteenth century, Catholics numbered ove
50,000.

After defeating the Portuguese in 1605, the Netherland
East India Company enforced the principle, then practice
throughout Europe, of *cuius regio eius religio*—believer
embrace the faith of the civil authority, which in the Indie
was Reformed Christianity. Partly for political but also fo
religious reasons, the company prevented the further sprea
of Roman Catholicism.

Nevertheless, Catholicism did not completely disappear
During the third period of Catholic history in Indonesia
1800–1945, the colonial government, applying the comity
principle, permitted Catholic missionary activity at firs
only in those areas already cultivated, notably on Java
Flores and north Celebes. For a time there was conflic
between government and church over the appointment and
status of priests, whom the government wished to contro
as it did the clergy in the Protestant church, but by 1847

Roman Catholic efforts to administratively separate church from state were successful and Catholic missions went forward actively. Educational work was especially emphasized by various religious orders whom the Jesuits, bearing main responsibility for Indonesia, invited to assist them.

The period since Independence has seen remarkable growth in the Roman Catholic Church, due in part to the extension of religious liberty to all. This has meant freedom to work anywhere in Indonesia and, like other recognized religious groups, eligibility for government aid to the educational, charitable and sometimes even religious work of the church. Theological education and the training of native clergy received special emphasis, to redress the heavy predominance of Europeans among the clergy and lay orders. The following statistics were given for 1964:

> Catholics totaled about 1.5 million concentrated on the island of Flores. . . . There were 30 bishops (4 native), 1,356 priests (220 native), 700 brothers (272 native) and 3,270 sisters (1,360 native). Catholics maintained 3 universities, with more than 7,000 students. . . . 2,414 elementary schools with 403,760 students; 520 secondary schools with 101,075 students; 49 normal schools with 4,950 students; 134 professional schools, with 10,200 students; 77 hospitals; and 68 orphanages. There were 20 minor seminaries, with 1,780 students, and 3 major seminaries for secular clergy and 8 for religious, with a total of 360 seminarians.[1]

Like the Protestant churches, the Roman Catholic Church in Indonesia has played a significant role in national affairs. A vigorous Catholic party (*Partai Katolik*) and a number

[1] *The New Catholic Encyclopedia.* New York: McGraw-Hill, 1967, VII, 480–81. Used by permission.

of Catholic mass organizations mobilize youth, university students, women, laborers, artists and farmers for political action. Catholics are represented in both legislative and executive branches of government. Catholic publications include a daily paper in Djakarta, three weekly magazines and six monthlies.

The Roman Catholic Church is a vigorous, widely dispersed, solidly rooted, actively engaged segment of the total Christian community in Indonesia. In recent years, especially since Vatican II, contacts and cooperation between Catholic and Protestant leaders have multiplied greatly and show bright promise for the future.

HOW PROTESTANT CHRISTIANITY CAME

The first period of the church's history in Indonesia, that of Roman Catholicism under the Portuguese, has been discussed. During the second period (1615–1815), the Dutch East India Company introduced Protestant Christianity to the areas it administered, mainly the Moluccas and the cities in western Indonesia. The company church, however, served primarily the employees of the company, using the Dutch language. Only peripheral attention was paid to Indonesians. One significant event for the spread of Christianity in Indonesia was the publication and distribution by the company in 1733 of the first translation of the Bible into the Malay language.

During the third period (1815–1930), the company church became a state church—still controlled completely by the Dutch government. At the same time, Dutch, German, Swiss and American missionary societies secured permission from colonial authorities to work in assigned regions. By the end of the nineteenth century, the Protestant

Church of the Indies[2] was no longer the only Protestant church in the archipelago. Missionary efforts planted and nourished more than 30 regional churches, most of which became autonomous after 1930. During the Japanese occupation and the revolutionary struggle (1945–49), practically all foreign assistance and control were removed from the Indonesian churches, for the first time in their history. Although this experience brought great hardship, it also facilitated self-government, self-support and self-propagation.

The fact that Indonesian Christians joined their fellow citizens of other faiths in the nationalist struggle against colonial subjugation did much to remove the stigma of "foreignness" that had adhered to Christianity. The Christian faith became an officially accepted religion in the Republic of Indonesia, based on the *Pantja Sila* (Five Principles, the first of which is "belief in God"). Immediately after Independence, Indonesian churches began to grow in numbers as well as in the depth and spread of their influence on Indonesian life. In both of these respects, Indonesian churches presently constitute the most vigorous and fastest-growing churches in the world.

WHAT KIND OF PROTESTANT CHRISTIANITY?

The Protestant churches in the DGI are described one by one in another book by this writer.[3] Here they can only be pictured in general terms.

[2] This is the official name of a church body, including the four regional churches in the Moluccas, Timor, Minahasa and western Indonesia. It is to be distinguished from "the Protestant churches" which denotes all the member-churches in the Indonesia Council of Churches, and some outside, in contrast to the Catholic Church.

[3] Frank L. Cooley, *Indonesia: Church and Society.* New York: Friendship Press, 1968.

Of the 38 churches in the DGI, at least five originated within or close to the Protestant Church of the Indies and its predecessor, the Dutch East India Company Church. The others, resulting from missionary activity, did not grow up in the bureaucratic, colonial atmosphere of the old state church, and hence they appear more vigorous, missionary minded and flexible.

In ecclesiastical tradition, the majority are Calvinist. Three have Methodist background, two are Mennonite, three come from the Pentecostal tradition and two are related to the Lutheran World Federation. In terms of membership, then, perhaps three million council-related Indonesian Protestants, or three out of four, come from the Calvinist branch of the Reformation.

In terms of origins the great majority, perhaps 25 churches, grew from Dutch missionary activities. At least four have relationships with German churches, three grew out of American missionary efforts and one from Swiss labors. Several are completely indigenous.

To picture the theological complexion of Indonesian churches is difficult. There are no "liberal" churches, in the American sense. Most are orthodox, strongly traditional and fairly inflexible in outlook. Those in the Pentecostal, Methodist and Mennonite families tend to be less conservative in spirit. A generalization that held true until recently would be: theology is for the church and is not related to the secular life of the world.

Twelve of the churches might be called "folk churches," while 22 others can be termed "gathered churches." Folk churches are the Christian communities in areas where a majority of the ethnic group has accepted the faith, coming out of animism into the church. A "marriage" has occurred between the ethnic culture and the Christian faith, for example, in Minahasa and Batakland. Gathered churches exist in situations where the Christian community comprises a small group gathered one by one from the majority adhering to the dominant faith which the church has not yet penetrated significantly, as in Javanese Islam and Balinese Hinduism.

A last perspective on the Indonesian churches would reveal that about one-third of the member churches in the Council serve people living in towns or cities and two-thirds serve people in rural areas. A still higher percentage of the local congregations are rural. The Protestant churches thus reflect faithfully the urban-rural balance in Indonesia.

The different churches are one manifestation of Christ's church in Indonesia. There is another equally important manifestation, namely, the varied forms of ecumenical cooperation in mission and service.

THE ECUMENICAL MOVEMENT AMONG PROTESTANTS

The ecumenical movement in Indonesia is a fruit of the missionary outreach of the church. The two earliest manifestations of ecumenical cooperation were the Missions Consulate (*Zendings Consulaat*), established in Djakarta in 1906 by the Netherlands Missionary Council as a liaison between churches and missions and the colonial government, and the Indonesia Bible Society, established in 1814.

The ecumenical movement in Indonesia has many manifestations. The Indonesia Council of Churches (*Dewan Geredja-Geredja di Indonesia*, or DGI), representing 38 member churches, is the largest ecumenical agency of Protestants. There are organizations serving functional needs, such as the Bible Society, the Christian Publishing

Body, a Christian political party and some mass organizations. Finally, there are specialized institutions that meet particular needs in church and society.

The Indonesia Council of Churches

Most Indonesian churches became autonomous before the Japanese occupation and the revolutionary struggle. This development, along with others, hastened the establishment of the Council of Churches in 1950. Preparatory experiences came from nearly 50 years of cooperation through the Missions Consulate, more than a century of work by the Bible Society, and participation in conferences of the International Missionary Council and the World's Student Christian Federation as early as 1928. Equally important, however, was the experience of national unity in the revolutionary struggle for freedom. The same forces that moved diverse peoples and separated regions into a unified national state were also at work in the Christian community.

First steps toward ecumenical cooperation were taken in 1946 by the churches in west, central and east Java, and early in 1950 by churches in the Celebes. The organizing assembly of the DGI was held in May 1950 in Djakarta. There, the 27 church bodies that became charter members set as one aim a unified Protestant church in Indonesia.

The development of the DGI is inseparable from the course of the nation's life since 1950. Changes in political systems, regional rebellions, steady economic decline, radical politicizing of life, all have affected the growth of the council. These turbulent developments have accentuated, more than was originally anticipated or perhaps desired, the role of the council in relation to the government and society. It sometimes appears, at least to those outside it, to be a "super-church" representing Protestant Christianity in Indonesia.

At the Council's Fifth Assembly in 1964, the number of member churches increased to 35, with the applications of several others pending. Organizationally the council is divided into five departments: mission and evangelism, service, unity, research, and church and society. Each department directs and supervises the work of several commissions.

The functions of the DGI are varied. It was envisaged as a center of conversation, planning and decision making for member churches. It was also to be a means to the realization of Christian unity. To a degree the second should grow out of the first. The council through its departments and commissions should assist member churches in particular program areas, especially mission and service, in utilizing the fruits of research and in developing resources, particularly personnel and facilities. The DGI serves as a liaison between member churches and various branches of government, an important function in light both of the somewhat unique relation between religious bodies and the government in Indonesia, and of the pace and scope of political change taking place. The Council of Churches also functions as a bridge between overseas and Indonesian church bodies, including such ecumenical bodies as the World Council of Churches and the East Asia Christian Conference.

Other Ecumenical Agencies

Several ecumenical agencies or enterprises are closely related to but not organically part of the DGI. These agencies represent efforts of Indonesian churches, in cooperation with overseas Christian agencies, to serve the churches and society in Indonesia in specialized fields.

The *Badan Penerbit Kristen* (BPK), literally Christian Publishing Body, continues the Dutch and German mission publishing agencies in Indonesia. It is owned, managed and staffed by Indonesians, and directed by an autonomous board of trustees. The BPK maintains close cooperation with the DGI and the Committee on World Literacy and Christian Literature (LIT-LIT) of the National Council of Churches in the U.S.A. The staff is headed by Mr. Alfred Simandjuntak, a Batak Christian who is a gifted linguist and musician besides being recognized as one of the ablest men in the publishing business in Indonesia.

In 1965 the BPK published 137 titles in the fields of theological and biblical studies, Christian ethics, youth problems, religious education for church and schools, family life, health, drama and fiction. About half the publications were translated works, with the rest being written by Indonesian authors. The BPK sponsors programs to stimulate and develop writers in Indonesia. With the literacy rate skyrocketing, as it did from below 20 percent in 1950 to 65 percent in 1965, the need for Christian literature is increasing much faster than the BPK's capacity to meet it.

The *Lembaga Alkitab Indonesia* (LIA), Indonesian Bible Society, which began in 1814 as the Java Auxiliary of the British and Dutch Bible Societies, was incorporated as a national Bible Society in 1951. Governed by its own board of directors but cooperating with the DGI, LAI performs three functions of crucial importance to the Christian movement in Indonesia—the translation, printing and distribution of the Holy Scriptures.

An ecumenical team of translators has been working since the early 1950's on a modern Indonesian version of the Bible, to replace the existing translation, which was prepared during the last century before the establishment of Indonesian as the national language. The changes that have taken place in the Malay language of that time to the Indonesian of 1968 are at least as great as the difference between the English of the King James Version and the New English Bible. The new translation should be ready by 1970.

The Bible Society has produced whole Bibles in seven regional languages in addition to the national language. New Testament translations are produced in 10 regional languages while Bible portions are available in 29 different languages. Indonesia's seven million Christians in a population of 112 million reflect the size and importance of the Bible Society's task.

The Student Christian Movement of Indonesia, GMKI, was organized in 1932 and since the late 1940's has been a member of the World Student Christian Federation. Rapidly growing, with 45,000 members in 72 local groups at present, the GMKI is the sole ecumenical outreach of witness and service to Indonesian students and teachers.

The PWKI, the Indonesian Christian Women's Association, has performed a similar function. It has been the channel through which women from the various churches throughout the country cooperate in expressing their common concerns.

GAMKI, the Christian Youth Movement; PERTAKIN, the Christian Farmers' Association; LKIK, the Christian Institute for Culture; and KESPEKRI, the Christian Labor Union, are examples of mass organizations that became active under "guided democracy" as Christians sought to influence public affairs.

MPPK, the Christian Schools Council, is the instrument of the extensive school systems operated by the regional churches on government subsidy, and in many areas it is the only educational facility available.

In another sphere Christians have developed new forms of mission. With the inauguration of "guided democracy" by President Sukarno in 1959, the political role of functional groupings in society became much more significant. Two new entries were registered in Indonesia's dictionary of acronyms: PARPOL, political parties, and ORMAS, mass organizations. Each religious or ideological group had its own party and adjunct mass organizations as instruments for the political mobilization and direction of its constituency.

PARKINDO, the Protestant political party, was born out of the revolutionary struggle that followed the 1945 Proclamation of Independence. Though not one of the largest parties, Parkindo has played a significant role both nationally and regionally. At least one Parkindo representative has served in every cabinet since 1945. In the 1955 parliamentary elections, Parkindo polled over one million votes, winning six seats. Being a small party, its policies have tended to be a response to positions and initiatives taken by its main challengers, the Muslim and Communist parties. Under these conditions it is natural to find Parkindo untiringly defending the Pantja Sila (Five Principles), foundation of the Indonesian state, which guarantee religious liberty for all.

Two other new forms of mission have appeared in the field of mass communications. *Sinar Harapan* (Ray of

Hope) is a daily newspaper published by a Protestant group as a medium through which a Christian voice can be heard in secular society and news of the Christian movement can be spread throughout Indonesia. Since it was launched in 1961, *Sinar Harapan,* with a daily circulation of 90,000, has become one of the three or four best dailies in the capital city. *Ragi Buana* ("Leaven of the World") is a monthly magazine of the *Reader's Digest* type, published since 1963 by the same group. The content is of general interest, always including at least one or two articles relating to the Christian faith or the work of the churches, articles of informational and educational value, poetry, short stories and biography.

The problems and opportunities connected with Christian political parties and mass organizations are reflected in the following sentences from the Message of the Central Committee of the DGI on October 13, 1966:

> After analyzing the present problems concerning the Church, political parties and mass organizations, we emphasize the following: (1) the Church is not a political party or a mass organization and may not be identified with a political party or mass organization; (2) still their members are called to be faithful and obedient witnesses of Christ in the midst of society, nation and state, both as individuals and as organizations; (3) the Church is called to serve, to give guidance, instruction, counsel and where needed, warning to its members who are members both of the Christian Political Party or Mass Organizations.

HIGHER EDUCATION AND CLERGY TRAINING

Prior to Independence in 1945, there was not a single university in Indonesia. Twenty years later the Ministry of

Higher Education listed 156 private and 78 public institutions of higher education with a student enrollment of about 250,000. Today there are several Protestant universities, enrolling more than 5,000 students.

The three that are well established and have received government certification reflect the patterns of Christian education. Nommensen University, sponsored and controlled by the Batak Protestant Christian Church in North Sumatra, was founded in 1954 in cooperation with the Lutheran World Federation. Established later the same year in the nation's capital was the Christian University of Indonesia. This institution, with six faculties and nearly two thousand students, is operated by a foundation composed of prominent Protestant leaders. *Satya Watjana* Christian University in central Java was inaugurated in 1956 as a normal school to train teachers. It is an ecumenical effort sponsored by 18 Indonesian church bodies in cooperation with overseas churches in Holland, Germany, Australia and New Zealand, as well as in the United States through the United Board for Christian Higher Education in Asia. In 1966 it enrolled 1,000 students, more than half from regional churches. In its 10 years of service, Satya Watjana has sent hundreds of alumni back to their home regions, especially to east Indonesia, to upgrade and expand the educational ministry of their churches.

Many of the 1,880 ministers serving member churches of the DGI are products of theological schools established before World War II. On this broad base, the 10 theological schools in Indonesia have developed along two lines. Churches in the Moluccas, Minahasa, Kalimantan and West Irian have established schools for the training of their own clergy. Other schools are jointly sponsored. In North Sumatra e Batak and Methodist churches have joined in developing the theological faculty in Nommensen University. A second union effort in theological education, serving students from 16 churches, primarily in east Indonesia, is in Iakasar. Established in 1953, with an enrollment of 118 udents in 1967, this Theological School of East Indonesia recently raised its standards to include instruction at the college level.

Duta Watjana Theological School in Jogjakarta is the youngest of the union institutions. This school, like the others mentioned, is sponsored and directed by Indonesians, ut fraternal workers from abroad help in providing instruction and in developing the school.

The Higher Theological College (STT) in Djakarta is the oldest and most ecumenical of the seminaries. From its inception in 1935, STT has been an ecumenical effort to serve the whole Christian movement in Indonesia. At present its student body numbers more than 160.

The American churches' emphasis in ecumenical cooperation in Indonesia has been concentrated on programs to train pastors and teachers for Indonesian churches.

THE LIFE AND MISSION OF THE CHURCHES

In 1966, following the abortive coup on October 1, 1965, with its bloody aftermath involving hundreds of thousands f Communists and suspected sympathizers, Indonesia entered a new phase of its revolution. Its leaders speak of a new order" replacing "the old order" that brought political conflict, economic disintegration and spiritual frustration to the people. The leaders of "the new order" have given priority to the goals of political stability and economic rehabilitation.

How do Indonesian Christians respond in this new period of challenge and opportunity? How do they see their missionary task?

One response, already clear and vigorous, has been to express by words and deeds the *dimension of witness* in the church's mission. New expressions of witness take two forms.

First, Indonesian church leaders are keenly aware of the need for Christian witness in the social, political, economic and cultural spheres of life. How is the word of God relevant in nation building in the crises of power, the horror of massacre, the struggle against injustice and oppression? A message from the Central Committee of the DGI, on September 11, 1966, addressed to Indonesian churches and society, dealt forthrightly with these issues:

> The Church has been placed by God in the midst of the peoples, nations and societies to carry out its prophetic calling, which means the obligation to express what is in keeping with, and what is contrary to the will of God in the life of a people and state.
>
> The participation of Christians in efforts to restore the life of our state and society must . . . be positive and creative . . . critical and realistic . . . because we know that injustice and oppression basically are rooted in the heart of man himself.
>
> In light of our experiences with the use and misuse of power, we must be keenly aware that power is needed in every society . . . to establish justice, to punish evil and to serve the welfare of the people. Since this power is always held in the hands of sinful men, in employing it man is always threatened by the danger of misusing it for personal interests of those of one's own group. . . . Every holder of power is continually threatened by the danger of

losing his humility and becoming arrogant. Consequently, we need to remember that the opportunity to use power is a gift of God who demands faithfulness and continuous self-criticism.

Second, in the area of personal evangelism, accounts have been coming in that suggest an almost unprecedented situation in various regions. Thousands of people are presenting themselves for instruction in the faith and baptism into the Christian community. Some come out of disillusionment with traditional faith (animism, Hinduism or Islam); some out of fear of being branded atheist (Communist); some out of awareness of need for direction and lasting values in a time of revolutionary change; some out of recognition that for man on his own (secularism and communism) there is no salvation, no hope, no joy, no strength to go on in suffering and frustration; and some because of what they have seen in Christians.

From the village of Tigalinga in northern Sumatra, for example, 15 ministers from six different communions joined in baptizing more than 2,000 people one Sunday in June, 1966. Several local congregations in central Java have doubled their membership during 1966. The General Secretary of the DGI, the Rev. S. Marantika, after giving instruction to a group of former Communist leaders in a Djakarta prison, baptized more than 20 in October, 1966. In some areas the number of people registering for instruction and baptism is so large that local congregations have mobilized everyone available to provide the needed ministry. Primary emphasis, it appears, may need to shift for a time from evangelism to Christian nurture, in order to meet this situation responsibly. Everywhere the need for leadership is increasingly felt.

The tide of Christian witness, both personal and social, is flowing strongly and authentically in Indonesia today. Every indication points to an increase of witness, which must surely lead to renewal. The theme of the Sixth Assembly of the Council of Churches on Reformation Day, 1967 in Makassar was "Behold, I make all things new" (Rev. 21:5), with "The renewal of man, church and society" as subtheme.

In its 1966 Christmas message the council said,

> Therefore, let us press forward firmly in our efforts to renew both our private life and the structures and values in the political, social, economic and cultural fields. Thus we can be saved from irresponsible, insensitive and hypocritical living, as well as from new forms of injustice in society. In the midst of the wrestlings of our people concerning the reality of the new humanity, new society, new world, the Church must be aware that it can only make a contribution if the repentance begins with the Church itself. The Church must renew its own life, its own faith, its own faithfulness to the Lord of the Church, Jesus Christ.

The *dimension of service* in mission is the second part of the response of Indonesian Christians to the new opportunities and needs. For more than ten years the DGI's Interchurch Aid Commission, in cooperation with various national church world service agencies, has been helping people caught by catastrophe—drought, famine, flood, earthquakes, volcanic eruptions and epidemics. Within the last few years the program has begun to include some pilot projects to stimulate local initiative in economic development. There is increasing need for this kind of physical rehabilitation through projects to increase agricultural production, to develop home and village industries, to provide assistance for family planning programs, public health and the like. Aid from outside can accomplish significant, though limited, objectives. Indeed, foreign aid may harm more than help, if it is not administered in such a way as to develop local initiative, self-respect, creativity and new skills. The Interchurch Aid Commission, in cooperation with Church World Service, will place more emphasis on economic development in an expanded program for the immediate future.

The *dimension* of *unity* is the third part of response. Ever since its creation, the DGI has wrestled with the task of furthering unity among the churches. There have been some encouraging advances, but no significant breakthroughs. On the contrary, in at least one region, northern Sumatra, there has developed since 1963 a schism in the largest communion in Indonesia.

Barriers to church unity in Indonesia as elsewhere are as much sociological and cultural as theological and ecclesiastical. This being the case, they are not significantly reduced by study papers in the Commission on Unity or by lectures on the floor of General Assembly. What can reduce them is increasing common efforts by the churches in witness and service. Evidence over the past two years (1966–67) suggests that this is beginning to happen in certain places. One concrete example is the growth of regional councils. For some years there has been talk of organizing regional councils of churches, but only since the Fifth Assembly of the DGI in 1964 have these intentions begun to materialize. Within the last two years regional councils have begun to function in north Sumatra, west Java, central Java, Kalimantan, north Sulawesi and the Moluccas. No financing has been available from the DGI, so they are completely dependent on regional resources. This may guarantee that structure and program grow out of needs felt in the regions. This development could have major positive influences on the DGI and on the movement toward unity.

Another development could have even more pronounced effects. The DGI-called Consultation on Unity in March, 1967 formulated a proposal on unity for submission to the Sixth General Assembly of the DGI in November, 1967. If approved, the DGI would be replaced by an Ecumenical Synod representing all member churches. A common Confession of Faith and Book of Liturgies would be used by all. Decisions on matters of general concern would be binding on all. After earnest study, the Sixth Assembly voted to defer action until 1970, to allow for further study, revision and reaction by the member churches. This remarkable proposal has advanced the movement for unity to a new stage of development, the most serious and significant of its kind thus far in Indonesia.

In conclusion, two aspects of the life of the churches, finance and leadership, relate particularly to their missionary response in the new situation. The numerical strength of the Indonesian churches does not reveal much about their strength in leadership and finance.

Under colonial rule the financial needs of the Protestant church were largely provided by the colonial government. Churches under missionary societies also received financial subsidies from overseas. Consequently, there was no stimulus for members to grow in stewardship. Contributions and offerings were made, but they were either symbolic or for some local purpose such as repairing a church. The program of the congregation was not felt to be the responsibility of the members. After Independence, however, outside subsidies were sharply reduced or cut off altogether and this forced the development of stewardship to meet the minimal needs of the local budget. But little is given for the wider work of the church. Most ecumenical enterprises and agencies still rely heavily on support from abroad. This is a source of present, as well as potential, problems. The challenge to mission demands greater attention to this aspect of the life of the church.

So too under colonial rule the leadership of the churches was the responsibility of foreign missionaries. Indonesian workers were trained before 1940, but seldom to be more than assistants. Since Independence a heartening growth, both quantitative and qualitative, has occurred in theological education, and the situation in Christian higher education is even more encouraging. Nonetheless, at present almost every church in Indonesia faces a crisis in leadership. First, there are not enough ministers to serve the existing congregations, especially in light of exploding new growth. Hundreds of teachers of the Christian faith are needed, because public and parochial schools are required by law to provide religious instruction to students from first grade through university. The Armed Forces have requested 300 more Protestant chaplains to serve the military establishment—one of the most promising missionary opportunities today. In many churches older ministers are reaching retirement age faster than young ministers can be educated to take their place. Leadership generally is still in the hands of older men trained under colonial conditions, who follow a traditional pattern of leadership that is no longer adequate in the rapidly changing scene. Serious tensions frequently develop between older and younger ministers.

TWO LEADERS

These comments are not meant to suggest that Indonesian churches are without leadership. Christ has raised up some striking figures in his service there. But the present level of challenge and opportunity calls for many more men like the Rev. T. P. Pattiasina and the Rev. Ardi Suyatno.

Thomas Pattiasina grew up in a small village on one of the "Spice Islands," an area which has been Christian for more than three centuries. After graduating from high school in Ambon in the late thirties he journeyed to Batavia, then seat of the colonial government, to enter the Higher Theological College, the first university-level theological course in Indonesia. Here he met students from other areas of Indonesia, and the growth process from Ambonese to Indonesian began. The Japanese occupation and the revolutionary war provided the setting, and participating in the struggle for independence comprised his extracurricular activities. Upon graduation Thomas married the daughter of a Dutch Indonesian family and the newlyweds sailed back to the Spice Islands, as a honeymoon trip. East Indonesia was still under Dutch rule and Tom, whose sympathies were with the Republic of Indonesia fighting for liberty, soon incurred the wrath of the Dutch Moderator of Synod for suggesting that the Moluccan church should begin to create a fund against the day when the state subsidy to the church would be cut off. This was judged an expression of disloyalty and insubordination, and the young minister was defrocked. Just as this occurred, he was discovered to have leprosy, which was interpreted as proof of his guilt. His young wife took a job and they moved to a tiny hut behind the Ambon marketplace where for five years they suffered physically and spiritually until God gave release from the disease and with it a new mission: to struggle for the renewal of the Protestant church of the Moluccas.

Tom Pattiasina had plenty of time to reflect on the dynamic changes in newly independent Indonesian society, in which the forces of secularism, Islam and communism were bringing a vigorous challenge to his tradition-minded, spiritually prostrate church. Concluding that the Moluccan church had to become a missionary church or disappear, he set himself the task of bringing a new direction and a new spirit—both from God—into the oldest Protestant church in Asia. And today, 10 years after his return to full-time ministry, the Moluccan church has taken several giant steps toward reform and renewal under his leadership. The Rev. Mr. Pattiasina is hardly known outside of the Moluccas because he has not once left his post in Ambon since 1947. Yet he is one of the foremost of Christ's saints in Indonesia.

Ardi Suyatno, a second-generation Christian, is also a graduate of the Higher Theological College. He was tempered in the fires of the revolution as a member of PETA, the Students' Army that fought against the return of the Dutch to Java in 1945. In his early forties, he was elected Moderator of the Synod of the Church of East Java. Before assuming this heavy responsibility, Ardi had served as general secretary of the commission on mission of his church, leading the work of bringing Christ to the 26 million Islamic believers of east Java, the area served by the 60,000 member Protestant church. His job has been to train and direct laymen to witness and serve in the areas immediately surrounding their congregations. Ardi himself served as pastor of a city church where young professional people, youth and students comprised an important part of his parish. Under Ardi's courageous and creative leadership, the east Java church has grown at a rate of several thousand adult baptisms and confirmations annually, in a region where Islam, Javanism and communism have been particularly strong and active. This shepherd of his flock, in the heat of conflict and terror following the October, 1965 coup, led his church in saying to Indonesians and to us all:

A Christian is one who is called by the Lord Jesus, not only to wait for gifts or beg for blessings, but also to participate in the work of the Lord in calling the world back to the sphere of the authority of the Kingdom of God. So the Christian is commanded to go out from his own safe and peaceful community, to join in hearing the abuse of Christ, in hailing the advent of the new order, in becoming the living stones in the upbuilding of the house of mankind in the power of the spirit.

6 THE PHILIPPINES

bulwark of the church in asia

Gerald H. Anderson and Peter G. Gowing

THE PHILIPPINES is the only Christian nation in Asia, with about 92 percent of its 35 million people adhering to the faith. In 1565, Spanish *conquistadores* and friars established Spanish rule and the Catholic faith in the archipelago, and at present 82 percent of the people in the land belong to the Roman Catholic Church. Some 5 percent belong to the Philippine Independent Church, a twentieth century schism from the Church of Rome; about 3 percent —somewhat more than a million persons—are Protestants, and the remaining 2 percent belong to the Iglesia ni Cristo and other indigenous Christian sects and cults. The nearly two million Muslims of the southern Philippines constitute the largest religious minority in the country, and there are still hundreds of thousands of tribal pagans in the mountain regions of Luzon, Mindanao and other large islands. small number of Buddhists are found among the Chinese

Filipinos, predominantly Malay in race, are descendant of migrant peoples who came to the archipelago before th time of Christ. Islam began a vigorous expansion amon them a century prior to the arrival of the Spaniards, but majority of the people were animists and spirit worshiper when the Europeans came. The Tagalogs and the Visayan had developed rather complex polytheistic religions, how ever, displaying Hindu-Buddhist elements that were prob ably mediated through contact with the Indianized civiliza tions of ancient Indonesia.

Spain ruled for three and a third centuries and in tha time halted the advance of Islam, containing it in th southern islands. She built a Christian, Hispanized civiliza tion in the central and northern parts of the archipelago Roads were constructed, agriculture and trade were stimu lated, education up to the university level was introduce and provisions were made for public health and welfare Negative aspects of Spanish rule included the use an abuse of forced labor for churches and public works, eco nomic exploitation and the denial of political and religiou freedom.

The Spanish language and the Catholic faith did muc to unite the linguistically and culturally diverse Filipino into a nation. In the nineteenth century, Filipino national ism, influenced partly by political liberalism emanating from Europe and nurtured in Masonic lodges, the Kati punan and other secret societies, challenged Spanish co lonial policies. Indeed, the Filipinos were in the midst o armed revolt against Spain when the Spanish-American War occurred in 1898. By the terms of the Treaty of Pari

(December 10, 1898), the United States assumed sovereignty over the Philippines; but for three years American troops were obliged to fight Filipino revolutionists who vainly sought the independence of their country from foreign rule. The Americans proved generally beneficent rulers, however, and from the beginning set about the task of preparing the people for self-government. The Philippine Commonwealth was inaugurated in 1935, giving Filipinos complete charge over their internal affairs and promising them full independence in 10 years. Despite World War II and the Japanese occupation there was no delay in carrying out that promise: On July 4, 1946 the Republic of the Philippines was proclaimed.

Two decades after Independence, the Philippines stands as a working model of democracy in Asia. Plagued by such problems as poverty among the masses, unemployment and underemployment, a small but troublesome Communist insurgency (*Huks*), corruption in high and low places, and a population explosion of dangerous proportions (an increase of at least 3.3 percent per year), the Republic nevertheless has the economic, political and social potential to deal with these challenges. The Christian church, Catholic and Protestant, is in a special position to assist the young nation in creating the moral and spiritual climate necessary, and to help raise up the dedicated and imaginative leadership required, to realize that potential.

ROMAN CATHOLIC CHRISTIANITY

Spanish Catholicism

In the sixteenth century, Spanish missionary friars brought to the Philippine Islands the light of the Christian gospel in the lamps of their Hispanized Roman Catholicism. They succeeded marvelously well in converting a population scattered in thousands of small settlements on hundreds of islands. Within a century of the arrival of the Spaniards, the majority of Filipinos had responded to the gospel and submitted to baptism. Only the hostile pagan tribes of Mountain Province and the Muslim (Moro) peoples of the southern islands resisted conversion to any appreciable degree. Elsewhere splendid churches and *conventos* rose to dot the land; Christian schools were founded; printing presses produced Christian literature in the native languages; Christian music and art were cultivated; Christian virtues and standards of conduct were inculcated; and the priests of the Catholic Church sought to soften the harshness of Spanish conquest. The Mass replaced pagan rituals; the *santos* (carved images of the Christian saints) replaced idols; prayers and novenas *for* the dead replaced prayers and sacrifices *to* the dead; the *fiesta* replaced pagan revelry; *Bathala,* the supreme diety of the old pagan polytheism, came to be understood as God the Father; and the pagan *simbahan* came to be regarded as the house of the Lord.

As time passed, however, the fine work of the early friars began to be compromised by the weakness of men. The church and the colonial government quarreled, and sometimes their differences flared into violence as they competed for influence and control in the islands. Friars quarreled with the growing secular clergy, and they refused to surrender their parishes to the latter as the law of the church required. And the friars refused to submit to the annual parish visitations of their bishops, also required by church law. The parishes grew large and wealthy, and some of the friar pastors grew fat and lazy. They also became greedy

ıd oppressive toward the tenant farmers who tilled the
ıil for them. The friar orders came to be powerful po-
ically and economically, and instead of ministering to the
elfare of the Filipino people, they came to be ministered
ıto. For the most part Filipinos were excluded from mem-
ership in the friar orders, partly for political reasons and
ırtly because of racial prejudice; and though they were
lmitted to the secular clergy, they rarely rose above the
ınk of parish assistant. No Filipino ever became a bishop
ı Spanish times. In the nineteenth century, when Philip-
ıne nationalism emerged in response to democratic ideal-
m abroad in the world, the Roman Catholic Church and
ıe friars generally were on the side of conservatism and
ıaction and stood opposed to the national aspirations of
ıe people. The friars became the objects of scorn to such
aders of the new nationalism as José Rizal, Marcelo H.
ɛl Pilar, Isabelo de los Reyes and Apolinario Mabini. It
ɛcame part of the program of the Philippine revolution of
ȝ96–1902 to expel the friars from the islands, to distribute
ıeir land to the tenant farmers, to give their parishes to the
ɛcular clergy, to Filipinize the Catholic hierarchy and
ɔ separate church and state.

eformation

In the nearly seven decades of the twentieth century, the
ɔman Catholic Church in the Philippines has undergone
considerable reformation. Under the American regime she
ɾas disestablished and learned to be virtually self-support-
ıg. She learned to adjust to the policies of separation of
ıurch and state and religious liberty. She was obliged to
ɔlerate the existence of the newly arrived Protestant de-
ɔminations, and she had to endure the schism of the

Philippine Independent Church. Surviving an initial perio
of bitter anticlericalism, she reorganized for the new da
She conscientiously recruited and trained more Filipir
clergy and raised Filipinos to the episcopate. She invite
religious clergy from other lands to undertake specialize
ministries under strict supervision and to carry respons
bility for new missions among the non-Christian tribe
She developed programs of social welfare and gave cor
siderable attention to deepening the spiritual life of th
masses of her lay faithful. She suffered terribly durin
World War II, but recovering quickly she has moved o
from strength to strength. Some 82 percent of the Filipir
people today owe allegiance to the Roman Cathol
Church. In 1960, the Archbishop of Manila, the Most Re
Rufino J. Santos, became the first Filipino member of th
Sacred College of Cardinals, a sure sign that the church i
the Philippines has come of age.

Present Condition

The Roman Catholic Church is in a generally robust cor
dition in the Philippines at the present time. This is not t
say that she is without serious problems. She suffers from a
acute shortage of clergy—in 1967 there was only one pries
for every 5,472 Catholics, one of the lowest ratios of priest
to lay people of any nation on earth. She is troubled by th
nominalism of much of her membership. In 1965 a mission
ary priest in Manila reported that "67 percent of all Fil
pinos live in Catholic families in which nobody goes t
Mass on Sundays . . . [and] at most 3 percent of all Fil
pino families are regularly practicing Catholic families.
The church is beset by what is sometimes called "folk
Catholicism—lingering elements of pre-Christian spiritism

d folkways conjoined to a superficial veneer of Catholic
lief and devotion. Moreover, the church is somewhat
oubled by the charge of "religious colonialism" based on
e fact that about 43 percent of her 4,418 priests are aliens,
any of them in key positions in her institutional life. The
urch continues to feel the challenge of other competing
hristian bodies: the Independent Church has sprung to
w life in recent years; the various Protestant denomina-
ons are very much alive and growing; and the powerful,
ighly nationalistic sect, Iglesia ni Cristo, is rapidly gaining
herents. Indeed, the Iglesia, founded in 1914 by an ex-
oman Catholic, Felix Manalo, who proclaimed himself as
e "fifth angel" of Revelation 7:2 and taught peculiar uni-
rian doctrines, is one of the fastest-growing religious
odies in the nation, gaining many of its converts from the
oman Catholic Church. Organized along rigidly authori-
rian lines, it claims two million members (most authori-
es would place the actual figure at about 700,000) and
xercises a marked influence in Philippine politics.

Despite these challenges, the Roman Catholic Church is
cing the future with apostolic zeal in every dimension of
er life. Her priests are being better educated and her peo-
le better instructed than ever before. She is learning to
ccept what she cannot change; and at the same time she
discovering new ways to witness in a rapidly changing
nd and society. In 1968, she has an estimated membership
f 28,700,000 persons—and the resources and energy of this
ast body of faithful are being harnessed for political, so-
ial, educational and spiritual ends in an impressive array
f organizations and movements. The Legion of Mary, for
xample, reportedly has more chapters in the Philippines
an in any other land. Several million Filipinos are en-

rolled in the Barangay of the Blessed Virgin Mary, whic
stresses neighborhood processions, catechetical instructio
and pious devotions. The *Cursillo* ("little course") mov
ment has in very recent years caught hold among layme
in the towns and cities. By study and prayer they are redi
covering in small groups the social and personal relevanc
of the Christian faith. Already the movement is having
noticeable effect in quickening the social conscience an
spiritual pulse of the church. Under the aegis of the hie
archy such agencies and groups as the Catholic Action c
the Philippines, the Catholic Women's League, the Youn
Christian Workers and the Jesuit-led Institute of Soci:
Order also help keep alive the church's social concern an
implement its social message.

In two other areas of activity, education and mission
the Roman Catholic Church shows considerable strengt
at the present time. A total of 1,637 schools (164 of ther
colleges and universities) are operated by the church an
enroll approximately one million students. The majority ar
supervised by various religious (monastic) orders of me
and women; and the influence of such respected institution
as the University of Santo Tomas (Dominican) and Atene
de Manila (Jesuit) is felt widely throughout the country
The religious orders also have major responsibility for th
church's work in missions. The Oblates of Mary Immacu
late, for example, do splendid work among the Muslims o
Cotabato and Sulu Provinces in their "Notre Dame" schoo
system. And the Congregation of the Immaculate Heart o
Mary does equally admirable work in parishes and school
among the tribesmen of Mountain Province on Luzon
Moreover, an apostolate, coordinated by a special bishop
vicar general, is actively at work among the large Chines:

pulation of the country. And mission outreach now ex-
nds to lands beyond the Philippines as well. In 1966 there
ere 23 Filipino priests and 240 nuns at work in such coun-
ies as Indonesia, Taiwan, Japan, Brazil, Peru, Argentina,
igeria and India.

In fulfilling her life and mission in a changing Philip-
nes, the Roman Catholic Church has had to rethink some
' her attitudes, modify old habits and adopt new tech-
ques of mission and ministry. One of the most encourag-
g developments was the National Congress for Rural
evelopment, sponsored by the Catholic hierarchy and
ld in Manila, Los Baños and Cagayan de Oro City, in
ebruary, 1967. The congress brought together 400 dele-
ites to ponder the plight of the 70 percent of the Philip-
nes population living in the rural areas who are faced
ith problems of poverty, illiteracy, malnutrition, inefficient
rming and fishing methods, and insufficient government
d private assistance. The congress is regarded as an im-
ortant step in developing concrete lines of action for the
urch to pursue its ministry to rural people.

Another very encouraging development is the new cli-
ate in Catholic-non-Catholic relations. The Pontificate
f Pope John XXIII and developments in the Second Vati-
n Council have helped immensely in creating the con-
itions wherein, for the first time, Catholics and non-Catho-
cs in some parts of the Philippines find it possible to ex-
eriment with dialogue and cooperation.

THE PHILIPPINE INDEPENDENT
AND PHILIPPINE EPISCOPAL CHURCHES

The Philippine Independent Church had its beginnings in
e Philippine revolution when Father Gregorio Aglipay

assumed leadership of the Filipino priests who sympathize
with the revolt against Spain. Aglipay and his followers di
not wish to break with Rome but when, after the war,
became clear that the Pope was not going to take immed
ate action to redress the grievances of the native clerg
they felt obliged to form a schismatic church. In this the
followed the initiative of a zealous nationalist leader, Isa
belo de los Reyes, who at a meeting of the Democrati
Labor Union in Manila in August, 1902, actually pro
claimed the formation of the Iglesia Filipina Independiente
Father Aglipay became its first Obispo Maximo (Suprem
Bishop).

As the only institution to survive the revolution, this new
church sought to interpret the gospel's support of the na
tional aspirations of the Filipino people. At first it wa
remarkably successful and in its early years it won ove
25 percent of all the Christians in the nation, includin
many former Roman Catholic priests. Sometimes whol
parishes switched allegiance from the Roman Catholic t
the Independent Church.

But its success did not last long. In 1906 the Suprem
Court ordered the Independent Church to return the prop
erties it had appropriated from the Roman Catholi
Church. Thousands of its members, unable to endure sep
aration from the beautiful buildings in which their antece
dents had worshiped for generations, went back to Roma
Catholic obedience. The new church was left in a desperat
condition—short of clergy, decimated in membership, with
out funds, forced to worship in hastily constructed build
ings. Its leaders shaped a liturgy which, while retaining th
outward trappings of Catholic ritual, nevertheless em
braced a form of unitarian and rationalist theology. Th

church became embroiled in politics and the weightier matters of the gospel became lost in an all-absorbing interest in nationalism and a bitter anti-Romanism. In time, the church was shaken severely by internal tension and division.

Very early in its life, the Independent Church sought the friendship of the Protestant Episcopal Church, which was organized in the Philippines around the turn of the century. But the first bishop of the Episcopal Church's Missionary District of the Philippines (today called the Philippine Episcopal Church), the great Charles Henry Brent, genuinely believed that the Independent Church was nothing more than a front for nationalist extremists and he refused to have anything to do with it. Moreover, he was anxious not to antagonize the Roman Catholic Church, which he regarded as a sister Christian communion, and thus he devoted the energies of his mission to evangelizing the pagans and Moros, serving the Chinese in the Manila area and ministering to the American and British residents in the Islands.

Not long after the Second World War, Bishop Isabelo de los Reyes, Jr., son of the famous patriot and co-founder of the Independent Church, became *Obispo Maximo*. This far-seeing church statesman had never really accepted the ultraliberal views of his father or Bishop Aglipay and, finding that many bishops, priests and laymen within the church shared his sentiments, he began to reform the church along more orthodox lines. A thoroughly trinitarian *Declaration of Faith and Articles of Religion* were drawn up, and appropriate changes were made in the liturgy. Overtures of friendship were made to the Philippine Episcopal Church, now headed by the Rt. Rev. Norman S. Binsted, and this time they were cordially received. The two communions embraced each other as sister churches. In April of 1948, the Episcopal Church conferred the historic episcopate on three bishops of the Independent Church (including Bishop de los Reyes), who in turn "regularized" the orders of bishops, priests, and deacons throughout their church in accordance with Catholic belief. Independent Church priests, who from the beginning had been notoriously ill trained, began to receive their education in St. Andrew's Theological Seminary of the Episcopal Church in Quezon City. And in 1961 the two churches entered into a Concordat of Full Communion, wherein each church recognized the other as holding all the essentials of the Christian faith. At the present time both churches, under the guidance of a joint council, are exploring the spiritual and pragmatic implications of that concordat, and the future appears bright as they look for ways to strengthen each other in programs of cooperation and support in all phases of church life.

While some people in both churches hope that their present accord will someday blossom into a merger, such an eventuality is unlikely in the near future. Even so, their relationship has proven mutually beneficial. The Episcopal Church has found an open door for wider service in the Philippines, and the Independent Church has benefited from the counsel and resources of an older sister in the Catholic faith. Already important results have been seen in cooperative efforts in college work, religious education, parish and diocesan development, mission outreach and stewardship.

The contrasts between the two communions are striking. The Independent Church dwarfs the Episcopal Church in size. The 1960 Census reported 1,414,431 *Independientes,* comprising 5.2 percent of the population. As of 1965, the church had 38 bishops in 25 dioceses and 424 priests serving 459 parishes and 850 *barrio* (village) chapels. The church is made up almost entirely of lowland Filipinos, most of them in central and western Luzon, the Visayas and northern and eastern Mindanao. The Episcopal Church, on the other hand, reported only 61,837 baptized persons for the year 1966, served by three bishops (a diocesan and two suffragans) and 95 other clergy (one-third of them aliens) ministering to approximately 200 congregations.[1] Most of the Episcopal Church's membership is made up of highland Filipinos in Mountain Province, and lowland Filipinos in western Mindanao, with some congregations of Filipinos, Chinese and Americans in the Manila area. The Independent Church is financially poor and has little in the way of institutional work, save for a few privately owned schools to which it lends its name. The Episcopal Church, in contrast, has considerable institutional work of excellent quality —schools, hospitals, social service centers—all strategically located in Mountain Province, Manila and western Mindanao. While the Episcopal Church is becoming increasingly self-sufficient financially, it is still able to draw heavily on the resources of its parent church in the United States. Both the Independent and the Episcopal churches join in supporting Trinity College of Quezon City (2,043 students enrolled in 1967). Both churches have begun sending missionaries overseas—there are Independent Church priests

[1] In 1967, Bishop Lyman C. Ogilby, an American, resigned as diocesan bishop and was succeeded by Bishop Benito C. Cabanban. Bishop Ogilby's resignation was made in the interest of "Filipinizing" the top leadership of the Philippine Episcopal Church, which is now directed by two Filipino bishops.

in Hawaii and Episcopal Church missionaries in Malaysia.

The two communions have stretched out their hands in ecumenical fellowship with other denominations within and beyond the Philippines. The Independent Church is a full member of the World Council of Churches and the East Asia Christian Conference. Both churches have become members of the National Council of Churches formed in 1963; indeed, Bishop de los Reyes was elected its first chairman, and Bishop Cabanban its second chairman. Relations between the Roman Catholic Church and the Philippine Independent Church remain far from satisfactory in the islands, but it is not without significance that Bishop de los Reyes in 1964 was cordially received at the Vatican by Augustin Cardinal Bea, President of the Vatican Secretariat for Promoting Christian Unity.

THE CHALLENGE OF ISLAM

Muslim Filipinos (popularly called Moros) constitute the largest non-Christian minority in the Philippines. Nearly two million strong, they are found mainly in western Mindanao and the Sulu archipelago. The Roman Catholic Church has had mission work among them since the late sixteenth century, and today its mission is mostly under the direction of the Oblate fathers mentioned earlier. Their converts have been few in number.

Several Protestant groups have missions among the Moros, notably the Christian and Missionary Alliance which has work in Cotabato and Sulu; the Missouri Synod Lutherans who have a mission in the Lake Lanao region; and the Philippine Episcopal Church which continues to do some work among Moros in and around the cities of Zamboanga and Cotabato. The United Church of Christ in the Philip-

ines sponsors Dansalan Junior College in Marawi City
n Lake Lanao, which attracts a considerable number of
Maranao Moro students. The school is an outgrowth of
he work of Dr. Frank C. Laubach who in the 1930's
eveloped his now world-famous literacy methods as a
missionary among the Maranao Moros. Southern Christian
College, another school related to the United Church of
Christ, located at Midsayap, Cotabato, also attracts Moro
tudents living in the area.

Christian missions, Catholic or Protestant, have not been
ble to attract many Moro converts for the simple reason
hat Islam has a powerful political and social as well as
piritual hold on its adherents. And the fact that Christians
nd Moros fought each other for more than 300 years (as
pain sought to subjugate the southern islands) has left a
egacy of hostility that militates against any easy success
or Christian missions. Islam is not a rival to Christianity
nywhere except in the area of its concentration, and even
here the strength of the Moro population is being diluted
y the influx of Christian settlers from the northern and
entral Philippines. Even so, Islam has undergone a marked
esurgence among the Moros since World War II, and
he Muslims are becoming increasingly self-conscious and
olitically articulate. They are aided in this by Muslim
missionaries and visitors from abroad, notably from Egypt,
Pakistan, Arabia and Indonesia. Still, they welcome Chris-
ian institutions which promote literacy, education, health,
nd improved agricultural methods among them. And
xcept in those places where Christian settlers encroach on
what they consider to be Moro property, the Muslims today
re generally willing to tolerate Christians as their neigh-
ors.

THE PROTESTANT CHURCHES

History

The advance and achievement of Protestantism in th
Philippines has been remarkable, especially considering th
relatively brief period of its history. The first Protestan
missionaries arrived in Manila in 1899, when the Unite
States decided to retain possession of the islands followin
the Spanish-American War. Before that time, freedom o
worship and circulation of the Bible had been restricted b
the Spanish colonial government under pressure of th
Roman Catholic Church. But religious freedom and separa
tion of church and state, earnestly desired by the Filipin
people, were guaranteed by the American government.

In this new atmosphere of freedom, Protestant mission
aries were received by the Filipinos in general with courtes
and curiosity. They were welcomed as allies in the struggl
against spiritual imperialism and as friends of religious lib
erty. Literally thousands came forward for baptism (usuall
*re*baptism) and joined the Protestant churches. Thus, de
spite its brief history, Protestantism in the Philippines ha
experienced a rate of growth that is matched in Asia onl
by the Protestant churches in Indonesia and Korea; an
today there are more than a million persons in the Filipin
Protestant community.

During World War II, 80 percent of all Protestant churc
property was destroyed, congregations were scattered, man
members and ministers were killed and virtually all foreig
missionaries were interned by the Japanese. For the Filipin
Protestant community, just beginning to come of age i
1941, this was a serious setback. The years immediatel

ter the war were a time for reconstruction, renewal and
conciliation. The achievement of Philippine Independence
om the United States in 1946 ushered in a new era. The
otestant churches were challenged to find better struc-
res and strategies for the life and mission of the church
d to become responsible partners in the important task
 nation building. The extent to which this challenge has
en met in the years since Independence is not easy to
easure, but certain developments and directions in the
e of the churches may be mentioned.

onsolidation and Proliferation

One of the notable characteristics of Protestantism in the
ilippines from the beginning has been the movement for
operation and unity among the churches. Soon after
ilippine Independence this movement gained fresh im-
tus with the formation of the United Church of Christ in
e Philippines (UCCP) in May, 1948. This union brought
gether Disciples of Christ, Evangelical United Brethren,
ilippine (independent) Methodist, Presbyterian and Con-
egational church traditions, along with several indigenous
oups, and together they represent the largest Protestant
urch in the Philippines today.

For various reasons, several major Protestant churches
d not enter into the union, the largest of these being The
ethodist Church and the Convention of Philippine Baptist
urches. But all these churches cooperate in many ways,
pecially through the National Council of Churches in the
ilippines, which was formed in 1963. This council co-
dinates joint action and cooperative endeavor of seven
ember denominations: the UCCP, The Methodist Church,
e Convention of Philippine Baptist Churches, the Evan-

gelical Methodist Church (IEMELIF), the Iglesia Eva
gelica Unida de Cristo, the Philippine Episcopal Chur
and the Philippine Independent Church. The Nation
Council represents nearly three million Filipino Christia
and enables the churches to take a united stand on religiou
civic, moral and social issues in the nation. Through tl
council these churches operate a radio broadcasting ne
work, produce literature for Christian education, carry o
a ministry of social welfare in cooperation with Chur
World Service and cooperate with the Planned Parenthoo
Movement in the Philippines. Other cooperative Protesta
endeavors include Union Theological Seminary, Philippi
Christian College in Manila and the Protestant Chapel
the University of the Philippines. These Philippine church
are also active participants in the East Asia Christian Co
ference and the World Council of Churches. Dr. Enriqu
C. Sobrepeña, a leading figure in the UCCP, was a pione
in the formation of the EACC and became the first chai
man of that body at its inaugural assembly in Kua
Lumpur in 1959.

Thus we can say that the spirit of cooperation and unit
which has characterized Philippine Protestantism in gener
from the beginning, has since World War II and Philippi
Independence found new vitality and, favored by tl
worldwide ecumenical movement, promises to become dor
inant in the years ahead.

At the same time, however, we must take notice of
counterdevelopment in Philippine Protestantism, namel
the continuing proliferation of church and missiona
groups, especially those which are not inclined to coopera
with the established churches. In 1966 there were 3₇
Christian religious groups registered with the Philippi

government, 82 percent of which started their work after World War II. While it is true that 53 percent of all non-Roman Christians are represented in the National Council, it must also be recognized that the vast majority of Protestant groups are outside the council and that they are the fastest growing churches. The largest of these are Seventh Day Adventists, Churches of Christ, Association of Fundamental Baptist Churches, Christian and Missionary Alliance, International Church of the Foursquare Gospel, Assemblies of God and the Southern Baptist Convention. Thus, fragmentation of the gospel continues, and Protestants still face the problem of an inwardly divided Christian community.

Influence and Outreach

The influence of Protestantism in the Philippines has been much greater than its size would suggest. Protestants are included among the eminent leaders of the professions, among business executives and journalists, in labor organizations, education and the arts. They have served at all levels of political office, including members of the supreme court, in the president's cabinet, and as ambassadors to foreign capitals. In 1962, Protestants made up 10 percent of the Philippine Congress, and of the eight new senators elected nationally in 1965, the one who received the greatest number of votes was a Protestant. While the overall influence cannot be measured, it is clear that the reforming and liberalizing impact of Protestant Christianity has had its effect in the Philippines.

Protestant outreach in witness and service finds expression in a variety of forms, most notably in medical work and education. There are 17 Protestant church-related hospitals (1,500 beds) and 51 mobile and stationary clinics throughout the islands, cooperating through the Inter-Church Commission on Medical Care. In the field of education there are 47 member schools and nine affiliated schools in the Protestant-sponsored Association of Christian Schools and Colleges, with a total enrollment of more than 50,000 students.

Another aspect of outreach is the continuing work of Bible translation and distribution. The Bible is now translated and published, in part at least, in 45 of the 89 Philippine dialects and languages. In 1966 the Philippine Bible Society distributed 1,020,023 Bibles, Testaments, Scripture portions and selections. The YMCA, another nondenominational and nonsectarian movement, which like the Bible Society has had a notable history and influence in the Philippines, reported 33,400 members in 20 branches in 1966.

An encouraging sign of development and maturity in the Protestant churches is the growing sense of missionary responsibility as "sending churches" from the Philippines. Despite extremely limited resources of personnel and money, at least three of the Philippine Protestant denominations have become "sending churches" in the missionary enterprise since the 1950's. The UCCP has had a total of 25 missionaries serving overseas since 1953, of whom 13 are currently serving in such countries as Egypt, Ethiopia, Iran, Malaysia, Indonesia, Turkey, Thailand and the United States (Hawaii). The Methodist Church has had a total of 20 Filipino missionaries serving abroad, of whom eight are currently in service in Okinawa and Sarawak. The Seventh Day Adventist Church is especially noteworthy in this regard, having sent out 165 missionaries to many parts of the world since the early 1950's.

Ministers and Members

One of the basic strengths of the Protestant churches has been the education of their ministers. Especially since Independence in the Philippines, there has been a further upgrading of theological education with the realization that the "Bible School" approach is not adequate for preparing ministers to work in revolutionary Southeast Asia.

The major Protestant seminaries are at Central Philippine University in Iloilo City; Silliman University in Dumaguete City; and Union Theological Seminary near Manila. These schools, along with several other seminaries, have a total enrollment of more than 600 men and women who are preparing for full-time vocations in the churches. This does not mean that the churches are satisfied either with the quality or the quantity of candidates for the ministry. Poor financial support of pastors by their congregations and the comparatively low prestige of the ministerial profession in Philippine society contribute to the difficulty of recruiting for the ministry. Yet, despite these deterrents, there is a healthy ratio of approximately one full-time minister per 350 Protestants in the nation.

The largest Protestant denominations are the United Church of Christ, with 142,000 members; the Seventh Day Adventist Church with 100,000 members; and The Methodist Church with 70,000 members. Nearly all the Protestant churches have reported net gains in membership annually since the war. The 1960 Census of the Philippines reported a 76.7 percent increase in the number of Protestants over the 1948 Census (and, oddly, refers to Protestants as a "sect"). Yet the actual increase of the Protestant percentage of the population in recent years has been negligible.

Protestant growth today is barely keeping up with the rate of population increase and, for the present at least, it seems that the Protestant segment of the population in the Philippines has leveled off at about 3 percent. The chief sources of growth are the natural addition of children and conversions of nominal Catholics. There are a modest number of conversions from the pagan tribes, but almost none from the Muslims in the southern islands.

Nationalization and Indigenization

To a large extent, Filipinos now occupy the major positions of responsibility and authority in the Protestant churches and related institutions. All the bishops of The Methodist Church and the United Church of Christ are nationals and, with very few exceptions, all the pastors of local congregations in these two large denominations are Filipinos. Missionaries for the most part serve in supporting and specialized capacities, while Filipino churchmen rightly dominate the decision making.

If a distinction can be made, however, it must be said that the significant advance toward nationalization within the churches has not yet been matched by a corresponding achievement of indigenization. Although Filipinos are now generally at the head of the Protestant churches, these churches and their related institutions are still heavily dependent on support from the United States. Part of the reason is that a burdensome American pattern of organization and administration, adopted by the early missionaries, has been carried over. It is a pattern of organization that the Philippine churches can ill afford. Many pastors are so poorly supported by their congregations (the average Methodist minister's salary is $23 a month) that they must supplement their income by other part-time employment. Inadequate stewardship is a major problem of all the churches, and there is a need to rethink the pattern of pastoral service and support in the local churches.

Theology, worship and organization—all are duplications of American types, not always good duplications or duplications of the best in America. Churchmen in other Asian countries sometimes complain that the Protestant churches in the Philippines are not truly a part of the church in Asia, but are simply appendages or extensions of the churches in America because of the dominating influence of and dependence on the United States (95 percent of the 1,400 Protestant missionaries in the Philippines come from the United States). Many Filipino Protestants recognize a measure of truth in this complaint, and some prefer it that way. But increasingly, especially among the younger leaders of the churches, there is a conscious sense of identification and partnership with the churches in Asia as well as in other parts of the world. Filipino churchmen are now giving significant leadership to the life and thought of the World Council of Churches and the East Asia Christian Conference, and there is a growing realization of the "oneness" of the church in its mission to the world.

New Forms of Christian Service in Nation Building

Twenty-three miles south of Manila, along one of the few paved national highways, is the *barrio* of Palapala, flanked by glossy green rice paddies, coconut palms, banana trees and colorful explosions of poinsettias that grow to roof level. There are 97 houses and 644 persons in the *barrio*. The adults in the *barrio* have an average of 4.3 years of schooling; nearly all the land is owned by two persons;

the majority of the residents are tenant farmers; and the average income per person is $70 a year (the national average per capita income is $140 a year). Most of the houses are constructed of bamboo and thatched nipa palms; only 33 houses have electricity, 9 have indoor toilets and none have screens. The water supply comes from two sources, a spring and a well, and is carried to most of the homes in buckets. There are 37 radios, 27 sewing machines, one piano and no telephones in the community.

Palapala is one of 28,000 *barrios* in the Philippines, and among the most urgent and staggering tasks facing the nation are agricultural training and rural development in these communities. According to a recent report, "Only one out of 6,666 college students is in an agricultural school; far too many prefer the prestigious—and overcrowded— white collar and professional courses. Antiquated and super- stitious methods of farming are a continual drag on the national economy."

Near Palapala the churches have established an agency devoted to dealing with these problems. The National Rural Life Center, sponsored by the National Council of Churches and Union Theological Seminary, started in 1963 a program of livestock production and agricultural training, with the assistance of Heifer Project, Inc., and Church World Service. The center trains pastors, seminary students and farmers in agricultural skills, in knowing the rural community and in getting acquainted with various govern- ment agencies that assist in rural community development. Along with the International Institute for Rural Reconstruc- tion, another private agency near Palapala for training workers to assist in the development of *barrio* communities, the National Rural Life Center is seeking to help in nation building at a crucial point, where most of the people are, in rural communities. A similar program in the southern part of the islands was started in 1963, when a group of laymen and ministers founded the Mindanao Christian Service Foundation in cooperation with Southern Christian College at Midsayap, Cotabato.

Although the Philippines is still very largely an agricultural nation, the thrust toward an urban-industrial economy is rapidly developing, and Manila is the hub of this development. Manila is a city of nearly two-and-a-half million people, the center of commerce, government and education, the symbol of power, wealth and progress in the Philippines. Its skyline and suburbs impress the visitor, somewhat deceptively, as being a mirror of America. Manila has 50 percent of the industrial plants and industrial workers in the entire nation. It also has the worst slums and crime rate of any major city in Southeast Asia. In order to minister effectively in this situation, the Protestant churches are preparing their pastors and people for new forms of witness.

In a strategic section of Manila is the Methodist Social Center, with a multi-ministry of vocational training, counseling, relief, medical and dental aid, recreation and student work. Within an eight-block radius of the center there are more than 200,000 students living and studying in a variety of private colleges and universities.

Through its Division of Social Concern, the United Church of Christ has evolved several new programs of training and ministry in an effort to touch the lives of industrial workers and their families. One program is that of pastoral training, through urban and industrial life seminars, to understand the problems and possibilities of effective ministry in the expanding industrial cities of the nation. In these seminars ministers learn from experts about urban development and inner-city planning, new forms of city living, community resources and the church's role in industrial development. Sometimes a seminary student is prepared for a specific urban-industrial ministry, and part of his education includes an internship year or a summer of employment in a mine or factory where he is wholly involved in the life and environment of an industrial worker.

Other new programs of frontier ministry have been related to the miners and their families in the mountain city of Baguio; to the urban squatters who were removed from Manila and hastily resettled in an area known as Sapang Palay, 20 miles north of Manila; and to the Mindanao Federation of Labor. Each of these new forms of ministry has been an attempt to relate the mission of the local church to a changing Philippines.

PROTESTANT-ROMAN CATHOLIC RELATIONS

Until very recently, relations between Protestants and Roman Catholics in the Philippines were characterized for the most part by polemics and hostility. Catholics have resented the Protestant incursion into a country they had "Christianized" for over 300 years, and Protestants have generally viewed the conservative Spanish Catholicism of the Philippines as little more than a veneer spread over ancient paganism. A good deal of suspicion remains on both sides, to be sure, but in the new atmosphere following the Second Vatican Council Protestants are at last beginning to recognize their Roman Catholic brothers as Christians (hence they are overcoming the habit of referring to Catholic converts as "new Christians"); and Roman Catholics are beginning to accept the fact that Protestantism has had generally a constructive impact on Philippine society and is here to stay.

Surprisingly little ecumenical dialogue and significant encounter have taken place in the Manila area, but the farther away from Manila one travels in the Philippines, the better the ecumenical climate gets—a most ironic situation. Nonetheless, there is evidence of some improvement in the overall situation, as seen in the growing friendliness of Roman Catholic and Protestant clergy toward one another at the local level and the increasing number of contacts between them. Thus after seven decades of aridity in their relationships, a change for the better is emerging between Protestants and Roman Catholics, and anyone with a wet finger in the ecclesiastical wind can expect further showers of blessing for this rather dry aspect of the Christian story in the Philippines.

Despite the natural resources in this rugged chain of 7,000 islands, and its strategic significance as a bridge between East and West, the Philippines is a nation faced by some fundamental problems, to which the Christian faith must continue to address itself if the churches are going to be responsible and relevant in a revolutionary situation.

Perhaps of greatest significance: the Philippines is a nation in search of an identity and purpose within Southeast Asia. After occupation and control by Spain for 333 years and by the United States until after World War II —or as the Filipinos quip, "Three centuries in a convent and two generations in Hollywood"—the country is caught in a bewildering collision between modern aspirations and ancient attitudes.

The Philippines is also a nation in search of integrity and stability. Its reputation as a "showcase of democracy" where no president has ever been reelected for a second term is overshadowed by its infamy for graft, corruption, smuggling, bribery and inefficiency. Some political observers of Southeast Asia now question whether the system can ever be reformed from within and feel that time may be running out for democracy in the Philippines.

The hope for the future of the nation rests with a new generation of young leaders, in their thirties, who hold positions of responsibility and authority in government, industry, business, education and the church. A recent issue of *Asia Magazine* spoke of them as " 'The Lively Generation'—a go-getting generation that is coming to power with an ethic far removed from the lotus-life of the past . . . providing the vitality and the idealism for sustained national development." Mr. Jose Luna Castro, editor of the influential *Manila Times* and a former student at Union Theological Seminary, observes that "the municipal leaders who sat in rocking chairs in the 1930's and 1940's, exchanging town gossip, are now astir with new ideas. They now have the sophistication to understand that a sanitation campaign is more meaningful and far-reaching in significance than a barrio fiesta." The thoughtful Filipino today says, "Let foreign observers be patient with us. There must be time for attitudes to change. There are no shortcuts to political maturity."

The churches can provide the spiritual fiber that is needed to strengthen and hold the nation together in this difficult period of transition. The same power of Jesus Christ that has brought the Filipino millions into the "blessed company of all faithful people" is the power that can open new channels of service, explore new areas for witness and discover new ways to communicate the eternal good news.

CONCLUSION
Gerald H. Anderson

IN THE INTRODUCTION we spoke about the need of the churches in Southeast Asia to become more indigenous and to assume a role of greater responsibility and participation in the contemporary Asian revolution, especially in the affairs of nation building. Throughout the book, illustrations have been given of how the churches in nearly every country are now relating themselves in new ways to the life and thought of the nations, and relying to a greater extent on indigenous leadership and support. Likewise there is encouraging evidence of emerging new forms of Christian witness and service as the churches respond to what God is doing in contemporary Asian history.

At many points in this study mention has been made of the East Asia Christian Conference, an organ of continuing fellowship and cooperation among 87 church bodies in 16 countries bounded by the Karachi-Sydney-Tokyo triangle. Born and continued in the conviction that "the purpose of God for the churches in East Asia is life together in a common obedience to him for the doing of his will in the world" (Preamble to the Constitution), the EACC has had four assemblies (Prapat, 1957; Kuala Lumpur, 1959; Bangkok, 1964; and Bangkok, 1968) and operates as a regional agency within the framework of the wider ecumenical movement. Much of the creative ferment in the churches of Southeast Asia is fostered by the EACC and finds expression in it. One observer has described and assessed the role of the EACC as follows:

> Doing in Asia what neither a national council of churches nor the World Council of Churches can do, the EACC meets a new and important need. Among its member churches it has stimulated stewardship and the sending of Asian missionaries. It convenes special consultations on common concerns in mission which range from urban and industrial evangelism to home and family life. Despite the scope of its interests, the conferences it sponsors, and the considerable work it does . . . the EACC is *completely* decentralized. It has no headquarters building. There is no central EACC file. Its secretaries and committee chairmen are found in all parts of Asia. "This," says D. T. Niles, the EACC's general secretary, with a twinkle, "is the Asian way." [1]

The EACC is the great new fact of the ecumenical era in Asia. It is not so much an organization as it is a move-

---

[1] W. Richey Hogg, "New Thrusts in the Theology and Life of the Christian Mission," *Christian Mission in Theological Perspective*, ed. Gerald H. Anderson. Nashville: Abingdon Press, 1967, pp. 210–11.

ment to get at the issues and ideas which are at the crucial cutting edges of mission in Asia, and then to put pressure behind these ideas so that they become too costly for the churches to neglect. In addition to promoting the sending of Asian missionaries and Joint Action for Mission among the churches in Asia, the EACC has stimulated thinking in the following specific areas:

—the place of Christian institutions in a secular state;
—the relation between Christian education and lay training;
—church and society problems set within the context of the dialogue between Christians and men of other faiths; and
—joint action in theological education.

In theological education, the EACC cooperates with the Foundation for Theological Education in Southeast Asia, the Association of Theological Schools in Southeast Asia, the federated faculty of the Southeast Asia Graduate School of Theology, and the *South East Asia Journal of Theology,* all with offices in Singapore. Through the EACC a number of Asian students receive scholarships each year for study in Asian seminaries outside their own countries. On a broader scale, the EACC sponsored the first Asian Faith and Order Conference, at Hong Kong in 1966, on the theme "Confessing the Faith in Asia Today." There the delegates declared that: "For the churches in Asia to confess the faith means that they speak out of their oneness given to them in Jesus Christ and that they speak also out of their solidarity with the world in which they live."

The fundamental idea of Christian solidarity with the world had already been affirmed at the Kuala Lumpur

Assembly in 1959, when the EACC stated that it is the task of the churches to discern the presence of Jesus Christ in contemporary Asian history, so that they may respond to him and participate in his work for the world.[2] Thus, in response to the question, "What is God doing in and through the Asian revolution?" Mr. M. M. Thomas of India, a prominent participant in the affairs of the EACC, can say: "There is a general consensus among the churches of Asia that God in Christ is present in the Asian revolution and his creative, judging and redemptive will is its essential dynamic." [3] This is an exciting Christian interpretation of the Asian revolution—as articulated by Asian Christians themselves. It is an interpretation that requires the churches in this period of profound change to penetrate and participate in the Asian revolution—to provide a Christian presence where the action is, so that the incarnation becomes intimate.

Yet revolution is risky, both for individual Christians and cherished church tradition and structures. But how can Christians afford *not* to risk involvement in a revolution that is "the most dynamic factor in the history of the twentieth century," especially when they discern that God is already there in the midst of it and beckoning to them?

The story is told of a Filipino, hiding in his home during the battle for the liberation of Manila in February, 1945.

[2] *Witnesses Together,* The Official Report of the Inaugural Assembly of the EACC, Kuala Lumpur, Malaya, May 14–24, 1959. Rangoon: EACC, n.d., p. 60.
[3] M. M. Thomas, *The Christian Response to the Asian Revolution.* London: SCM Press, 1966, p. 27 *passim.* This is by far the most profound and provocative book on the subject by an Asian churchman, and the present writer is deeply indebted to it.

s the Japanese and Philippine-American forces exchanged
re in the street outside, he crouched below the windows
id listened to his battery operated radio. Suddenly he
eard an announcement over the radio that the Japanese
ad surrendered and that an armistice had been declared.
ut outside the fighting continued; the men in the street
ad not yet heard the news. The Filipino was then faced
rith a difficult decision: should he remain safely inside
rith the news of peace, or, at the risk of getting shot,
iould he go out and try to stop the fighting with the an-
ouncement of an armistice?

This is the dilemma faced by Christians in Southeast
sia—and everywhere—today: Can they enjoy the victory
nd peace of Jesus Christ in the safety and security of isola-
on from the struggles of society? Or *must* they carry the
rord into the conflict for world community in which all
ien are involved? The answer is clear. "For the Word is
ive, and love lives by going forth to be freely given." [4]

L. Harold DeWolf, "The Gospel, the Church, and the Mission,"
hristian Mission in Theological Perspective, ed. Gerald H. Anderson.
Iashville: Abingdon Press, 1967, p. 55.

SUGGESTIONS FOR FURTHER STUDY

Bibliography

Anderson, Gerald H. (ed.), *Christianity in Southeast Asia: A Bibliographical Guide*. New York: Missionary Research Library; and New Haven: Yale University Southeast Asia Studies, 1966. Paperback.

Maps

Atlas of South-East Asia (Introduction by D. G. E. Hall). New York: St. Martin's, 1964.

Map of the World's Religions and Missions, Martin Schlunk and Horst Quiring (eds.). Stuttgart: Evang. Missionsverlag, 1966.

General

Bastin, John, *The Emergence of Modern Southeast Asia: 1511-1957*. Englewood Cliffs, N.J.: Prentice-Hall, 1967. Paperback.

Bates, M. Searle and Wilhelm Pauck (eds.), *The Prospects of Christianity Throughout the World*. New York: Scribners, 1964.

Benda, Harry J. and John A. Larkin (eds.), *The World of Southeast Asia: Selected Historical Writings*. New York: Harper and Row, 1967.

Bone, Robert C., Jr., *Contemporary Southeast Asia*. New York: Random House, 1962. Paperback.

Burling, Robbins, *Hill Farms and Padi Fields: Life in Mainland Southeast Asia*. Englewood Cliffs, N.J.: Prentice-Hall, 1965. Paperback.

Buss, Claude A., *Southeast Asia and the World Today*. Princeton: Van Nostrand, 1958. Paperback.

Butwell, Richard, *Southeast Asia Today and Tomorrow: A Political Analysis*. New York: Praeger, 1964 (rev. ed.). Paperback.

Eastman, Addison J., *This Is Southeast Asia Today*. New York: Friendship Press, 1968.

Goodall, Norman et al., *A Decisive Hour for the Christian Mission*. London: SCM Press, 1960.

Gordon, Bernard K., *The Dimensions of Conflict in Southeast Asia*. Englewood Cliffs, N.J.: Prentice-Hall, 1966. Paperback.

Haas, Harry, *Christianity in the Asian Revolution*. Baltimore: Helicon, 1966. Paperback.

Harrison, Brian, *South-East Asia: A Short History*. New York: St. Martin's, 1966 (3rd ed.).

Hunter, Guy, *South-East Asia: Race, Culture and Nation*. London: Oxford University Press, 1966.

Kahin, George McT. (ed.), *Governments and Politics of Southeast Asia*. Ithaca: Cornell University Press, 1964 (3rd ed.).

Karnow, Stanley, *Southeast Asia*. New York: Time, Inc., 1962.

Manikam, Rajah B. (ed.), *Christianity and the Asian Revolution*. New York: Friendship Press, 1955. Paperback.

Manikam, Rajah B. and Winburn T. Thomas, *The Church in Southeast Asia*. New York: Friendship Press, 1956. Paperback.

Niles, D. T., *Buddhism and the Claims of Christ*. Richmond, Va.: John Knox Press, 1967.

Rawson, Philip, *The Art of Southeast Asia*. New York: Praeger, 1967. Paperback.

Ripley, S. Dillon, *The Land and Wildlife of Tropical Asia*. Morristown, N.J.: Silver Burdett, 1965.

The South East Asia Journal of Theology, John R. Fleming, Editor. Singapore: quarterly, 1959 and following years.

Tarling, Nicholas, *A Concise History of Southeast Asia*. New York: Praeger, 1966.

Thomas, M. M., *The Christian Response to the Asian Revolution*. London: SCM Press, 1966. Paperback. (Distributed by Friendship Press.)

Vandenbosch, Amry and Richard Butwell, *The Changing Face of*

Southeast Asia. Lexington: University of Kentucky Press, 1967. Paperback.

Von der Mehden, Fred R., *Religion and Nationalism in Southeast Asia: Burma, Indonesia, The Philippines.* Madison: University of Wisconsin Press, 1963.

Weber, Hans-Ruedi, *Asia and the Ecumenical Movement: 1895–1961.* London: SCM Press, 1966.

Burma, Thailand, Vietnam, Cambodia and Laos

Anderson, Courtney, *To the Golden Shore: The Life of Adoniram Judson.* Boston: Little, Brown, 1956.

Brown, Robert McAfee, Abraham Heschel, and Michael Novak, *Vietnam: Crisis of Conscience.* New York: Association, 1967. Paperback.

Cady, John F., *Thailand, Burma, Laos and Cambodia.* Englewood Cliffs, N.J.: Prentice-Hall, 1966. Paperback.

Dournes, Jacques, *God in Vietnam: A Christian Mission on the Plateaux of Vietnam.* (English trans. by Rosemary Sheed.) London: Geoffrey Chapman, 1966.

Dowdy, Homer E., *The Bamboo Cross: The Witness of Christian Martyrs in the Communist-Infested Jungles of Vietnam.* New York: Harper and Row, 1964.

Fall, Bernard B., *The Two Vietnams: A Political and Military Analysis.* New York: Praeger, 1967 (2nd rev. ed.).

Hamilton, Michael P. (ed.), *The Vietnam War: Christian Perspectives.* Grand Rapids, Mich.: Eerdmans, 1967.

King, Winston L., *A Thousand Lives Away: Buddhism in Contemporary Burma.* Cambridge: Harvard University Press, 1964.

Smith, Donald Eugene, *Religion and Politics in Burma.* Princeton: Princeton University Press, 1965.

Thich Nhat Hanh, *Vietnam: Lotus in the Sea of Fire.* New York: Hill and Wang, 1967. Paperback.

Wells, Kenneth E., *History of Protestant Work in Thailand: 1828–1958.* Bangkok: Church of Christ in Thailand, 1958.

ingapore, Malaysia and Brunei

ornwall, Nigel Edmund, *Borneo: Past, Present and Future.* Westminster, England: SPG, 1953. Paperback.

umper, Anthony, *Vortex of the East.* London: SPG, 1963. Paperback.

ood, George, *Malaya: The Challenge.* London: Presbyterian Church of England, 1957. Paperback.

ees, Shirley P., *Jungle Fire.* London: Oliphant, 1964.

lilne, R. S., *Government and Politics in Malaysia.* Boston: Houghton-Mifflin, 1967. Paperback.

urcell, Victor, *Malaysia.* New York: Walker, 1965.

regonning, Kennedy G., *A History of Modern Malaya.* London: Far Eastern Universities, 1964.

ndonesia

ooley, Frank L., *Indonesia: Church and Society.* New York: Friendship Press, 1968. Paperback.

eith, Herbert, *The Decline of Constitutional Democracy in Indonesia.* Ithaca: Cornell University Press, 1962.

rant, Bruce, *Indonesia.* New York: Cambridge University Press, 1964.

litt, Russell T., *Cannibal Valley.* New York: Harper and Row, 1962.

Iolt, Claire, *Art in Indonesia.* Ithaca: Cornell University Press, 1967.

ahin, George McT., *Nationalism and Revolution in Indonesia.* Ithaca: Cornell University Press, 1952.

raemer, Hendrik, *From Mission Field to Independent Church.* London: SCM Press, 1958.

egge, John D., *Indonesia.* Englewood Cliffs, N.J.: Prentice-Hall, 1964. Paperback.

lcVey, Ruth T. (ed.), *Indonesia.* New York: Taplinger, 1963.

The Philippines

Anderson, Gerald H. (ed.), *Studies in Philippine Church Hi
    tory*. Ithaca: Cornell University Press, 1968.

Corpuz, Onofre D., *The Philippines*. Englewood Cliffs, N.J
    Prentice-Hall, 1965. Paperback.

Deats, Richard L., *Nationalism and Christianity in the Philip
    pines*. Dallas, Texas: Southern Methodist University Pres
    1967.

Gowing, Peter G., *Islands Under the Cross: The Story of th
    Church in the Philippines*. Manila: National Council c
    Churches in the Philippines, 1967. Paperback.

Phelan, John Leddy, *The Hispanization of the Philippine
    Madison: University of Wisconsin Press, 1959.

Ravenholt, Albert, *The Philippines: A Young Republic on th
    Move*. Princeton: Van Nostrand, 1962. Paperback.

Sobrepeña, Enrique C., *That They May Be One*. Manila: Unite
    Church of Christ in the Philippines, 1964 (rev. ed.). Paper
    back.

Whittemore, Lewis Bliss, *Struggle for Freedom: History of th
    Philippine Independent Church*. New York: Seabury Press
    1961.

ABOUT THE CONTRIBUTORS

ERALD H. ANDERSON

Pennsylvania-born Gerald H. Anderson has been a Methodist issionary since 1960 in the Philippines, where he is professor church history and ecumenics both at Union Theological eminary near Manila and in the federated faculty of the Southast Asia Graduate School of Theology. A former Fulbright holar, he has studied at the universities of Marburg, Geneva nd Edinburgh, and has degrees from Grove City College B.S. in Commerce) and Boston University (S.T.B. and Ph.D.). e was a visiting scholar at Union Theological Seminary, New ork, in 1965–66 and a summer visiting professor at Garrett heological Seminary in 1966.

Before going to the Philippines he served for three years as ssociate minister of a Methodist church in Providence, Rhode land, where he met his wife, Joanne (also the author of a riendship Press book on children in the Philippines). The ndersons have two children.

Dr. Anderson is widely known as the editor of four other ooks: *The Theology of the Christian Mission* (1961), *Sermons > Men of Other Faiths and Traditions* (1966), *Christian Mis*ion in Theological Perspective* (1967), and *Studies in Philip*ine Church History* (1968). His articles and reviews have ppeared in numerous Asian, European and American journals. le is co-editor, with Bishop Stephen Neill, of the *Concise Dic*ionary of the Christian World Mission,* to be published in 1969.

PAUL CLASPER

Since 1964 Paul Clasper has been professor of ecumenics and vorld religions in the Theological School of Drew University at Madison, New Jersey. Born in Ohio, he was educated at Taylor Jniversity, Southern Baptist Seminary and Union Theological

Seminary, New York (S.T.M., Th.D.), and served pastorate
in Indiana and Brooklyn. An ordained minister of the American
Baptist Convention, Dr. Clasper was a missionary to Burma
from 1952 to 1963, where he served as vice president of the
Burma Divinity School near Rangoon. He has been a postdoc
toral fellow at the University of Chicago, and a visiting pro
fessor at Andover Newton Theological School. His book *New
Life in Christ* (1961) was published in the World Christian
Books series, and he has contributed articles and chapters to
numerous scholarly publications.

FRANK L. COOLEY

Frank L. Cooley, a Presbyterian minister, worked in Peking
and Chungking, China, from 1946 to 1951 as student secretary
with the YMCA International Committee. Since 1955 he has
served in Indonesia through the Commission on Ecumenical
Mission and Relations of the United Presbyterian Church in
the U.S.A., teaching in Djakarta and Salatiga, Java, and since
1967, working on the staff of the Indonesia Council of Churches
with the Commission on Study and Research. A graduate of
Springfield College (B.S.) and Yale University (B.D., S.T.M.
M.A., Ph.D.), he has written a monograph on *Ambonese Adat*,
published by Yale Southeast Asia Studies in 1962, and a book
on the Christian church in Indonesia, *Indonesia: Church and
Society*, published by Friendship Press in 1968.

RENÉ DE ROECK

René De Roeck, a Belgian, studied philosophy and theology
at the University of Louvain. In 1950 he became a member of
the *Société des Auxiliaries des Missions* and was ordained a
Roman Catholic priest. He first went as a missionary to South
Vietnam in 1951, where he served as a teacher of science in
schools in Vinh Long until 1957 and as director of studies at
the University of Dalat until 1964. During 1964 and 1965 he

tended two sessions of the Second Vatican Council as secre-
ry of the Vietnamese bishops. In 1966–67 he was in Belgium
a the staff of the Catholic missions journal *Eglise Vivante*,
til he returned to his work in South Vietnam at the end of
)67.

AY C. DOWNS

Ray C. Downs grew up in northern New York State. He is a
:aduate of Columbia University, McCormick Theological Sem-
ary and Princeton Theological Seminary, and has done addi-
onal work at University of Michigan and University of Penn-
/lvania. He has worked as a Scout executive, camp director,
nd merchant seaman. Following his graduation from Seminary
e organized and served as first pastor of a new church in
idianapolis. Later, he worked with the Board of Christian
ducation of the United Presbyterian Church and was Director
: Youth Work in its Commission on Ecumenical Mission and
elations. He went to Thailand with his wife and family in 1949
 help the (United Protestant) Church of Christ in Thailand to
stablish student work. He is the founder of the Student Chris-
an Center in Bangkok, a project that combines many of the
spects of a student union, university housing unit and student
ffairs office. He also lectures in Chulalongkorn and Thammasat
Iniversities.

)HN R. FLEMING

John R. Fleming is executive director of the Association of
heological Schools in Southeast Asia, and of the Foundation
)r Theological Education in Southeast Asia (which succeeds
ie Nanking Theological Seminary Board of Founders repre-
ented in Asia by Dr. Fleming since 1957). He is also editor
f the *South East Asia Journal of Theology* and dean of the
outheast Asia Graduate School of Theology.

Theologically trained in Glasgow, Heidelberg and Union
heological Seminary, New York (Th.D.), he served his Church

of Scotland as a missionary in Manchuria from 1938 to 19
There he taught several years in the Moukden Theological C
lege of the Church of Christ in China. From 1952–58 he v
general secretary of the Malayan Christian Council, and c
currently taught in Trinity Theological College, Singapo
where he continues to reside.

PETER G. GOWING

Peter Gordon Gowing, a native of Massachusetts and a m
ister of the United Church of Christ, graduated from Bang
Theological Seminary and University of Maine, and has a Th.
in ecumenics and church history from Boston University as w
as a doctorate in Asian Studies from Syracuse University. He l
served as pastor of rural churches in Maine and as chaplain in t
United States Navy. A missionary of the United Church Boa
for World Ministries since 1960, he now serves as Professor
Christian History and World Religions at the Divinity School
Silliman University at Dumaguete City in the Philippines. He
the author of two books on Philippine religion, *Mosque and M*
(1964) and *Islands Under the Cross* (1967), and has co
tributed articles to such scholarly journals as the *South East A*
Journal of Theology, Philippine Studies, Church History a
Muslim World.